DOPAMINE DETOX:

The 7-Day Reset to Break Distractions, Reclaim Focus & Boost Productivity

Peakstate Protocols

FREE BONUS FROM PEAKSTATE PROTOCOLS

Greetings!

First, thank you for reading our books.

As a welcome gift we offer the Peakstate Protocols eBook Bundle for free. Plus, you can be the first to receive new books and exclusives! Remember it's 100% free to join.

Simply click the link below to join.

FREE DOWNLOAD

https://www.subscribepage.com/peakstate

Keep up to date with us on:

https://peakstateprotocols.com/

Contents

Introduction

Imagine this: It's your usual morning. You reach for your phone as soon as you wake up, just mindlessly scrolling through social media notifications and emails before even rolling out of bed. As you sip your coffee, news alerts and updates bombard you, quickly followed by the irresistible pull of those little red dots signaling messages and likes. Sound familiar? By the time you're supposed to be getting ready, your mind is already cluttered with an overwhelming amount of information, leaving you feeling anxious and distracted. You're not alone in this digital chaos.

Welcome to the modern struggle with overstimulation—a world where instant gratification and constant connectivity leave our brains craving more while paradoxically draining our focus and productivity. If you've ever found yourself endlessly procrastinating, jumping from tab to tab, or unable to resist the lure of your smartphone during work hours, it's time for a change. This book is your guide to breaking free from this cycle and reclaiming control over your mental space. "Dopamine Detox" provides a fast, actionable plan to detox from the overload and regain motivation. This book goes beyond the usual generic advice to explore the root causes of our digital addictions and mental obstacles. It features engaging stories, real-life case studies, and practical exercises aimed at reprogramming your brain for enhanced focus, deep work, and success.

Why should you care about a dopamine detox? Understanding how dopamine–the "feel-good" neurotransmitter–affects your brain can be the key to unlocking extraordinary levels of concentration and achievement. You'll learn how to channel your mental energy away from distractions and toward meaningful goals and aspirations. Whether you're aiming to excel in your career, master new skills, or simply be more present in everyday life, this book will provide the tools you need for a complete cognitive reset.

Within these pages lies a clear, structured 7-day or optional 14-day dopamine reset system tailored especially for high achievers, entrepreneurs, professionals, students, and self-improvement enthusiasts. It starts with identifying the underlying reasons why you're caught in the dopamine trap–those unconscious habits and societal pressures that keep you stuck in a loop of instant pleasures at the expense of long-term rewards.

Next, we'll uncover the solution through the framework of a dopamine detox, which balances actionable steps with scientific insights. No longer will you be a slave to the pings and dings that elicit quick doses of pleasure but rob you of lasting satisfaction. Instead, you'll find yourself rewiring your brain for enhanced productivity and unwavering self-discipline. This journey isn't about quitting technology completely; it's about mastering it so that it serves you, rather than consuming you.

As you progress, you'll also develop strategies to build a fortress against distractions that go beyond temporary fixes. This long-term strategy emphasizes resilience and proactive measures, enabling you to guard your newfound clarity and focus amidst an ocean of daily disruptions.

The end result? A life transformed through intentional living. Picture yourself accomplishing tasks you once deemed impossible because you now possess the mental toughness and discipline to tackle them head-on. Envision savoring each moment without the nagging urge to check your notifications, creating a harmonious balance in both personal and professional spheres.

Ultimately, my goal is to help you break free from distraction' chains by providing a comprehensive roadmap that guides you every step of the way. So, are you ready to step into a new reality where you can clear your mind, regain your focus, and sharpen your mental abilities to tackle any challenge? Welcome to your dopamine detox journey—a path to freedom from distractions and endless possibilities!

Chapter 1: The Problem—Why You're Stuck in the Dopamine Trap

The constant buzz of notifications, the irresistible allure of an endless social media feed, and the barrage of emails begging for immediate attention—sound familiar? In this digital age, it seems like everyone's fighting a battle with distraction. Imagine trying to settle down with a cup of coffee to focus on that project you've been putting off, only to be interrupted by the thrill of seeing a new Instagram like or the curiosity of checking just one more news headline. Before you know it, hours have slipped away, and you've barely scratched the surface of your work. This isn't just procrastination—it's a modern-day trap of fleeting dopamine hits that pull us from task to task without ever allowing us genuine focus.

This chapter explores why we often struggle with constant distractions and putting things off. We'll look at how today's distractions are not just wasting our time—they're affecting our ability to focus, making it hard to be productive, and stealing our clear thinking. By laying bare the reality of our fragmented attention spans, we'll examine the ways this dopamine-driven environment is affecting our lives and what steps can guide us back to a place of focus and calm.

The Impact of Modern Distractions on Focus and Productivity

In today's digital world, the constant sound of notifications has become a familiar background noise in our daily lives. These interruptions, birthed from the very technology intended to enhance our productivity, instead fragment attention and impede cognitive flow.

The Environment of Distraction

Research shows that smartphones and social media create an environment rife with interruptions, effectively redefining our work and study spaces as territories teeming with distractions. As attention spans dwindle, the ability to focus for sustained periods slips away, complicating our capacity to engage deeply with tasks and content.

The Fallout of Persistent Distraction

The fallout of persistent distraction is significant. First, we see a hindrance in task completion. The average attention span when engaging with a digital device has plummeted from roughly two and a half minutes in 2004 to just 47 seconds today (Oaten, 2024). This reduction in attention leads to increased errors as tasks are frequently interrupted and never fully absorbed or processed. Each notification and each switch in context stall momentum, sending the mind into a state of perpetual reset.

The Cycle of Procrastination

On top of these problems, constant distractions lead to increased procrastination. The appeal of quick digital rewards offers an easy way out of tasks that require our attention. Rather than engaging with challenging material—like a dense textbook or a complex project—students and workers alike are tempted to indulge in the instant validation offered by social media likes or a quick scroll through a newsfeed. This cycle leads to delays in work completion, which only fuels anxiety and pressure to meet deadlines at the last minute.

Elevated Stress Levels

These behaviors also elevate stress levels. Our brains, continually bombarded with stimuli and forced into frequent context switching, become overstretched. The constant need to adjust and reorient depletes mental resources and results in cognitive fatigue. Emotional health suffers, with stress manifesting as anxiety and contributing to a rise in cases of burnout among students and professionals (Oaten, 2024). As time goes by, the brain gets used to this new normal of distractions, making it hard to find the calm focus needed to stay engaged or to do deep work, which is essential for success in school and work.

Recognizing Disruptions

Recognizing these disruptions is a crucial first step in managing them. Being aware of how constant distractions can harm you can motivate you to adopt more focused habits. When you understand that these interruptions don't just take away seconds or minutes but also affect your overall quality of life and productivity, you're encouraged to make strategic changes. The impact of distractions isn't just about the time you lose; it's also about the depth of understanding and learning that you're sacrificing (Attia, 2017).

Practical Methods for Mitigating Distractions

Practical ways to reduce distractions include setting up structured focus periods. One effective method is the Pomodoro Technique, where you break work into short, focused bursts followed by short breaks. This technique helps you regain control over your attention, allowing for deeper engagement with tasks while respecting your brain's natural rhythms. When scheduling specific times for focused work and setting limits on interruptions—like silencing your phone or using tools that help you concentrate—you can take back some control over your attention.

Creating a Distraction-Free Environment

Additionally, setting up a distraction-free environment is also very important. Identifying specific triggers that lead to distraction, such as quick access to social media or open communication channels during work periods, enables individuals to develop tailored strategies to combat them. For instance, keeping phones out of sight during study sessions or using apps that restrict access to distracting websites can significantly improve concentration and task completion rates. These strategies serve not just to increase productivity in the immediate, but also to train the brain to sustain attention for longer periods, thereby rebuilding tolerance for deeper work.

Attention-Management Techniques

Cultivating better attention-management techniques—such as single-tasking, setting clear objectives, and allowing for regular mental breaks—also proves beneficial. Regular breaks are vital, not just for resting but also for refreshing cognitive resources. Activities like short walks, mindfulness exercises, or even simple breathing techniques can effectively "aerate" the brain, promoting clarity and facilitating sustained mental effort upon returning to the task at hand.

Moreover, understanding and being aware of these distractions is a vital step in exploring how the dopamine loop influences behavior. In our upcoming section, we will examine how dopamine—often referred to as the reward and pleasure chemical—shapes not only our behaviors but also our decision-making processes related to rewards.

Balancing Distractions and Productivity

As you look at distractions this way, you begin to understand how they are part of a bigger motivational framework that impacts learning and productivity. Recognizing and managing distractions isn't about trying to live without them;

it's about building the self-discipline to choose when and how they fit into your life.

Protecting Our Mental Landscape

Understanding the connection between external distractions and our internal desires is important for protecting our mental space from the dopamine-driven cycle of instant rewards. When we give ourselves moments of undisturbed focus and set aside time for productivity, we begin to break free from this harmful cycle. This leads to opportunities for greater efficiency and mental peace.

As we move through today's world, we can start to take back control of our attention by being aware and using practical strategies. This helps us find a balance between short-term pleasures and long-term benefits.

The Mechanics of the Dopamine Loop and Its Effects on Behavior and Reward-Seeking

We're often bombarded by distractions that pull us into the so-called dopamine trap, leaving us stuck in cycles of temporary pleasure that affect our focus and productivity. Previously, we examined how modern distractions such as smartphones and social media challenge our ability to concentrate, setting up a stage for the dopamine loop to thrive. Now, let's take a closer look at how this loop works as a key force behind our behavior and decision-making, often focusing on immediate rewards rather than lasting satisfaction.

Understanding the Dopamine Loop

The dopamine loop kicks in as modern distractions tease us with instant gratification, and this loop strengthens impulsive behaviors. Each ping from a phone or like on social media triggers a mini-reward system in our brains, encouraging us to repeat the behavior to get another dopamine hit. This cycle is detrimental because it reinforces the desire for immediate gratification at the expense of lasting satisfaction or achievement (Bromberg-Martin et al., 2010). Imagine scrolling through social media feeds for just a quick peek, only to find that hours have passed. These distractions create a feedback loop that siphons our attention away from meaningful activities, perpetuating the cycle of momentary pleasure.

The Addiction to Quick Rewards

Society's push for quick results has led to a widespread addiction to instant rewards. People hustle for immediate success, often at the cost of their ambition and aspirations. Examples like constantly checking emails to feel productive or purchasing unnecessary items for a fleeting thrill illustrate how embedded this addiction is in daily life. This behavior doesn't just diminish our focus—it undermines sustained motivation needed for achieving long-term goals, trapping us further in the dopamine loop (Volkow et al., 2010). When you focus on short-term wins, you often overlook long-term projects and relationships that provide deeper satisfaction and meaning.

Clouded Mental Clarity

Moreover, the dopamine loop significantly clouds mental clarity, making it difficult to discern beneficial distractions from harmful ones. For instance, taking a break to watch a short video can quickly turn into hours of binge-watching, with watchers justifying their actions as stress relief. The truth is that these behaviors strip away our ability to make sound decisions and keep us stuck in patterns that are anything but productive. Realizing this, it becomes crucial to break free from the constant cycle of seeking temporary rewards in order to regain mental clarity and make decisions, leading to genuine satisfaction (Bromberg-Martin et al., 2010).

Redefining Satisfaction

Understanding why we should reduce our reliance on immediate rewards brings us closer to maintaining a clear mind and forging paths that truly nourish our aspirations. When we simplify our context by allowing fewer opportunities for dopamine-triggering distractions, we can focus on activities that contribute to our long-term well-being. Whether it's dedicating time to meditation, physical exercise, or a creative pursuit, cultivating behaviors that eschew the need for constant rewards could significantly improve our mental clarity (Volkow et al., 2010).

A Shift in Perspective

The decision to step out of the dopamine loop isn't merely about abstaining from distractions; it's about redefining what satisfaction looks like. When we reevaluate our needs and focus on activities that promise long-lasting fulfillment, we begin to balance the scales. This shift requires a conscious effort to identify activities that resonate with our values, providing meaning beyond immediate pleasure. As you create spaces that reduce distractions and emphasize long-term commitments, you set yourself up for a more focused and intentional life.

The Broader Impact on Mental Health

Finally, understanding the wider effects of our dopamine-driven society helps explain why these loops make it hard to break free from addictive habits. The appeal of things that are new, fast, and instantly rewarding may provide a quick boost, but they often result in dissatisfaction and declining mental health over time. As we untangle the complicated relationship between dopamine and decision-making, we find a chance to use our brain's reward system for personal growth instead of feeling trapped (Bromberg-Martin et al., 2010).

With this understanding, we get ready to explore the nuances of dopamine imbalance and its effects on mental health in the next section. Linking the challenges of decision-making within dopamine loops to potential mental health issues underscores the importance of being aware of symptoms related to dopamine. This prepares us for deeper insights into spotting imbalances and understanding how they affect our ability to thrive. As we move forward, we will maintain our focus on strategies that encourage balanced dopamine interactions, which can improve overall well-being and productivity.

Identifying Signs of Dopamine Imbalance and Its Implications on Mental Health

Recognizing the Symptoms

Do you feel like you can't seem to get things done or stay motivated? This is one of the biggest signs of a dopamine imbalance. Dopamine plays a critical role in motivation, and when its levels are off, it can lead to symptoms like irritability, difficulty concentrating, and a lack of pleasure in activities that used to excite you. Recognizing these symptoms is the first step toward taking control and avoiding potential long-term mental health issues such as anxiety and depression.

The Productivity Impact

Dopamine imbalance doesn't just mess with your mood—it's a productivity killer, too. When you're trapped in constant distraction loops, your brain's reward system, driven by dopamine, keeps seeking immediate gratification instead of focusing on important tasks (Cleveland Clinic, 2022). This can leave you in a cycle of chronic inattention and procrastination, where long-term goals are sidelined for short-lived pleasures. The key lies in making lifestyle changes that bring your dopamine levels back into balance, helping you regain mental clarity and focus.

Effective Strategies for Restoration

Exercise is an effective strategy for restoring dopamine balance. Physical activity doesn't just improve your physical health; it also boosts your brain's dopamine production, lifting your mood and strengthening your ability to concentrate. Try committing to a regular exercise routine—a brisk 30-minute walk or a short workout session daily can do wonders. You'll notice an increase in energy and motivation, paving the way for better productivity and well-being.

Nutritional Support

Foods rich in magnesium and tyrosine, such as almonds, avocados, and bananas, serve as building blocks for dopamine production. Incorporating these into your diet contributes to natural dopamine generation, improving mood and motivation (Cleveland Clinic, 2022). Prepare meals with these ingredients to support mental clarity and maintain your focus on essential tasks.

Limiting Distractions

Limiting distractions is another critical step. The constant pings and dings from your phone or computer can keep your brain trapped in a loop of dopamine-driven anticipation for what's next. Set specific times to check emails and social media, and designate periods for focused work without interruptions. Over time, you'll create an environment that supports productivity, boosts concentration, and minimizes distractions related to dopamine.

Building Routines

Establishing routines can support emotional balance and protect against the dopamine trap. Having a consistent daily schedule helps train your brain to expect and reward productive, mood-boosting activities rather than impulsive distractions. Try starting your day with activities that energize and ground you—like exercise or reading—before diving into work tasks. This structure enhances stability and improves your ability to manage immediate gratification behaviors effectively.

Taking Breaks to Reset

Taking breaks during work can also assist in regulating dopamine levels. Your brain needs time to reset, so ensure you step away every hour or so for a quick break. Use this time to stretch, breathe, or take a stroll. You'll return refreshed and better prepared to focus, breaking the cycle of procrastination that a dopamine imbalance can fuel.

Seeking Professional Guidance

In some cases, professional guidance might be essential, especially if symptoms persist or worsen. Don't hesitate to reach out to a healthcare professional who can provide the support and treatment necessary. They can help assess whether an underlying condition significantly affects your dopamine levels and guide you in exploring more personalized solutions.

Fostering a Balanced Mindset

Implementing these lifestyle changes will help to balance your dopamine levels, which will further improve your mood and energy, while also boosting your ability to focus and achieve long-term goals. Embracing these practices will help you avoid the pitfalls of distraction and maintain a clear, balanced mindset. The key to escaping the dopamine trap lies in these simple but effective strategies that support both your mental health and productivity.

The Importance of Awareness

Awareness of your body's signals can't be understated. When you recognize the signs early and adopt practices that align with your needs, you're not just fixing what's imbalanced—you're preventing the deeper, long-term implications of unchecked dopamine fluctuations. This journey of self-awareness and intervention paves the way for healthier, more fulfilling lives.

The Power of Small Changes

Addressing this chemical imbalance does not require drastic changes. Small, consistent actions accumulate over time, leading to significant improvements. Incorporating activities that stimulate the body and engage the mind can weave a fabric of well-being—one that supports your ambitions without falling prey to distractions. Keep striving, and take charge of your dopamine through informed, thoughtful action, fostering both wellness and success.

With these practices, you harness dopamine's power, channel it effectively, and build a resilient foundation. As you progress, exploring new methods for enhancement and growth ensures that you always remain in tune with your mind and body's evolving needs.

Summary and Reflections

In today's digital world, distractions are everywhere, making it increasingly difficult for us to concentrate on meaningful tasks. Notifications from our phones, endless social media feeds, and the pressure to respond to emails constantly pull us away from our work. However, this issue extends far beyond simple procrastination; it's a pervasive cycle of instant dopamine rewards that leads to shortened attention spans and diminished productivity. As we delve into this chapter, you'll uncover how these distractions not only waste precious time, but also disrupt our ability to think clearly and engage deeply with our work.

The consequences of this constant barrage of interruptions are profound, resulting in prolonged procrastination and elevated stress levels. Many individuals find themselves feeling anxious and overwhelmed, struggling to keep up with their responsibilities as their mental resources become increasingly depleted. Understanding the impact of these digital disruptions is crucial for anyone looking to enhance their focus and reclaim their productivity.

Fortunately, several practical methods can help combat these distractions effectively. Techniques like structured focus periods, such as the Pomodoro Technique, can create a more manageable work environment, while setting clear objectives for tasks helps maintain direction. Additionally, fostering a distraction-free workspace and incorporating mindfulness practices, regular exercise, and a balanced diet can further support mental clarity and restore dopamine balance.

But what if the very wiring of your brain has been altered against you? What if the science of dopamine reveals deeper truths that could change the way you interact with the world? As we transition to the next chapter, prepare to uncover the intricate relationship between dopamine and your daily decisions, and learn how to effectively rewire your brain to reclaim your focus and intentionality. The revelations ahead may just challenge everything you thought you knew about your habits and behaviors—stay tuned!

Chapter 2: The Science of Dopamine: How Your Brain Got Rewired Against You

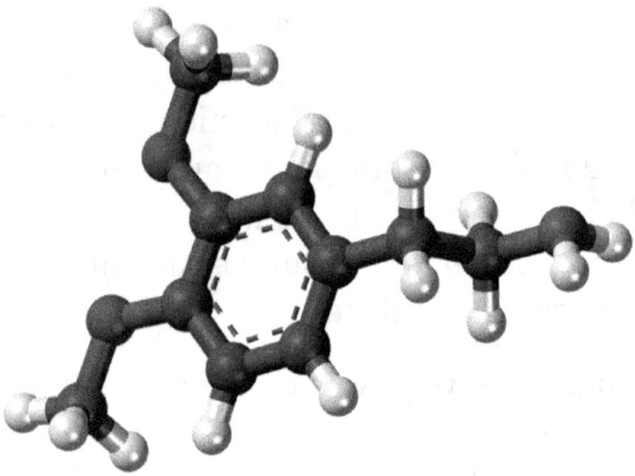

Have you ever wondered why it's so hard to stay focused, even when you're doing something you love? You sit down with every intention of working on that big project or diving into a good book, but somehow, distractions always manage to pull you away. Maybe it's the constant buzzing of your phone or the endless stream of social media updates that seems more interesting than what's in front of you. It feels like your brain is working against you, making it a challenge to concentrate and follow through on long-term goals.

Now, imagine having the tools to understand what's really happening inside your mind and how you can regain control over those distractions. This chapter will explore the invisible forces at play, specifically the role of dopamine, in steering our focus and motivation. As we dig deeper, you'll begin to see how modern life has rewired our brains and what steps you can take to reclaim your ability to concentrate, stay disciplined, and achieve what truly matters.

The Role of Dopamine in Motivation, Focus, and Discipline

Dopamine lies at the heart of the brain's reward system, a vital player in driving our motivation, focus, and discipline. For high-achievers and professionals, understanding dopamine's role in these processes offers valuable insights into managing behavior and productivity. When talking about dopamine, we're actually discussing two main types of signals in the brain. Some dopamine neurons are like motivational cheerleaders, excited by rewards and dampened by aversive events, steering us toward goals and boosting our evaluation of positive outcomes (Bromberg-Martin et al., 2010). Others shout out alerts every time something noteworthy happens, regardless of whether it involves a carrot or a stick.

The Impact of Dopamine on Behavior

But what does this mean for you? Imagine you're facing a big project. Those ambient cues associated with reward—perhaps a promotion—ignite your motivational fire. Dopamine levels surge, coaxing you to engage, strategize, and achieve. This dopamine-fueled drive is crucial, as it boosts your willingness to approach and complete rewarding tasks (Speranza et al., 2021). However, the benefits of dopamine depend on balance. A steady and controlled release of dopamine helps keep you motivated and focused, which is really important for staying disciplined over the long run.

Dopamine and Neuroplasticity

Think of dopamine as the manager of your brain's adaptability. As it influences neuroplasticity, it assists in learning and memory creation, engraving pathways that remind you what's worth chasing after. Repeatedly rewarding experiences sculpt these neural routes, streamlining effort toward productive ends. Yet, too much of a good thing—uncontrolled dopamine spikes—leads to impulsivity, pulling focus toward immediate gratification rather than the delayed rewards that discipline demands. Picture navigating a shopping spree, with dopamine dancing at every flashy sale sign, not with long-term savings in mind but with that immediate thrill of purchase. This impulsivity can sidetrack your road to success.

The Constant Battle Against Distractions

For high-achievers, the constant battle against distractions is all too familiar. Dopamine highlights adaptability, which is crucial for aligning your habits with achieving success. When dopamine channels rewards correctly, neural circuits are primed for enhanced focus and productivity (Bromberg-Martin et al., 2010). Conversely, inconsistent dopamine cues can result in scattered attention, with the brain ricocheting between tasks but settling on none. This tug-of-war defines the challenge of maintaining focus amidst a barrage of dopamine-triggering signals, from email pings to social media likes, which hijack attention.

The Rewiring of the Brain

But to truly grasp dopamine's impact, consider the brain's rewiring in response to consistent cues. The appeal of habits—like exercising regularly, picking up a new skill, or even putting things off—shows how dopamine shapes our behaviors (Speranza et al., 2021). When you regularly follow these routines, you create neural pathways in your brain that shape your habits and actions. This remarkable adaptability can either work for you or against you, depending on how you interact with these habits. It's a careful balance between the rewards of dopamine and the distractions it can amplify.

The Modern Landscape of Distractions

Most notably, today's environment is filled with stimuli, each one promising quick bursts of pleasure. The dopamine-driven cycle is relentless, nudging you from work to phone alerts and everything in between. These constant hits dilute your pleasure response over time, making common experiences less satisfying due to the brain's need for a more intense dopamine release to achieve the same sense of gratification. This quest for novelty leads not just to distractions, but also to a potentially reduced ability to sustain focus on any given task.

Strategic Management of Dopamine

However, there's hope in recognizing these patterns. Strategically managing dopamine, like through a dopamine detox, can help reset your dopamine response and assist in recovering from overstimulation. When you refrain from short-lived dopamine stimulation—by limiting social media and reducing digital noise—you allow your brain to resensitize and appreciate smaller rewards once more. This awareness doesn't just restore balance but also fosters a healthy alliance with dopamine, empowering you to harness its benefits without falling prey to its pitfalls.

Understanding dopamine's dual nature provides you with valuable tools. It's not about denying pleasure, but rather reshaping reward pathways to align with your long-term goals and enhance productivity. Being mindful of this balance translates to more robust performance narratives, where dopamine is not just the carrot that spurs you onward, but also the anchor that keeps you steady, adaptable, and strategically focused.

Recognizing these patterns and adopting strategies to counter their effects, like a dopamine detox, lays the groundwork for reducing procrastination and inspiring action. This understanding serves as a vital intervention, preparing you to navigate the challenges of constant distractions toward a more focused and fulfilling path.

How Overstimulation Dulls Pleasure and Kills Ambition

The Role of Dopamine

Dopamine acts as an essential component of our brain's reward system, integral to motivation, focus, and discipline. In the earlier sections, we discussed how dopamine fuels these drives, but there's a catch—overstimulation can dull its effect. When our brains swim in a sea of stimulation, thanks to high dopamine levels, it can ironically erode the very motivation it bolstered.

The Impact of Modern Overstimulation

The issue of overstimulation in our modern world often hinges on our infinite exposure to stimuli. Our daily lives are saturated with social media, streaming platforms, and an endless variety of entertainment options. This constant state of alertness and engagement doesn't just tax our attention; it diminishes our brain's pleasure responses. Over time, we demand more stimulation to achieve the same previous dopamine highs, leading to reduced dopamine sensitivity. Essentially, our brains become less responsive, necessitating an increase in pleasurable stimuli just to feel normal (Hu & Nguyen, 2022).

The Science Behind Pleasure Erosion

The science here is straightforward and disconcerting. Our brains get rewired so that activities or substances that previously brought joy no longer do. Our ancestors, in their primal existence, experienced stark contrasts between seeking and finding, fulfilling basic needs, and then resting. Today, however, that seesaw of pleasure and pain is disrupted as we're bombarded with nonstop dopamine triggers (Hu & Nguyen, 2022). When we're constantly exposed, our brains naturally adjust their thresholds, pushing us toward dopamine deficit states. It's a serious challenge:

these deficits can spiral into depression, anxiety, or something more subtle, like a pervasive sense of dissatisfaction.

The Erosion of Simple Pleasures

Imagine the difference in feeling after watching an episodic series for hours versus an evening walk. The TV show might entertain, yet perhaps not entirely satisfy in a lasting way. Meanwhile, a simpler experience like walking might increasingly feel mundane against the bells and whistles of digital media. The relentless quest for entertainment in our overstimulated brains leads to an erosion of our appreciation for simple pleasures (Cleveland Clinic, 2024).

The Cycle of Needing More

There's a significant issue here: the cycle of needing more to feel less. Modern stimuli not only make it difficult to experience happiness in simpler things, but also diminish our ambition. Before, a small win might inspire you to tackle bigger goals. Now, it's possible that pushing for more significant achievements becomes secondary to the pursuit of immediate gratification from a constantly stimulating environment. Actually, abstaining from enjoyable activities might sound joyless, but it can be a powerful tool against this overstimulation.

Breaking the Cycle

So, what's to be done? Breaking the cycle requires conscious effort. For some, exploring the concept of a dopamine detox might hold appeal despite some misconceptions about its execution. What's worthwhile instead is focusing on setting boundaries with technology. Intentionally reducing screen time or consciously choosing activities that don't bombard you with rapid-fire dopamine hits, like reading a book or cooking a meal.

Utilizing Cognitive Behavioral Therapy

Cognitive Behavioral Therapy (CBT) offers another avenue. This approach teaches how to sit with discomfort without reaching for an immediate fix. Instead of turning to screens or other stimuli to manage stress, consider getting comfortable with uncomfortable feelings (Cleveland Clinic, 2024). CBT guides individuals through specific strategies to tackle compulsive behaviors, using methods that do not necessarily involve cutting out enjoyable activities altogether. Through focused adjustments in personal habits, people might recapture some of the tolerance lost to overstimulation.

Rethinking Technological Engagement

Nevertheless, finding balance in this modern barrage isn't just individual work. Collectively, we need to rethink how to navigate technological engagement. Constant connectivity and digital notifications displace what's meaningful and fulfilling. As future sections will discuss, digital engagement, particularly through social media and gaming, intensifies the dysfunction in our dopamine systems. It's not merely exposure that impacts us, but also the quality and context of it. As suggested, this isn't solely an individual or societal problem; it's a combination that requires a nuanced strategy to embrace technology without relinquishing our ability to find joy in simple, meaningful experiences (Hu & Nguyen, 2022).

Focusing on these practical steps to restore dopamine sensitivity may lead to ways to regain lost motivation without the all-or-nothing thinking often seen in discussions about dopamine fasting. Our goal is to reshape routines while maintaining the role of pleasure, avoiding hedonistic behaviors that can derail our ambitions. It's about developing new patterns where balance becomes our ally as we navigate a dopamine-rich world with a healthier combination of simplicity and moderation.

The Real Cost of Social Media, Gaming, and Constant Notifications

The Overwhelming Digital Landscape

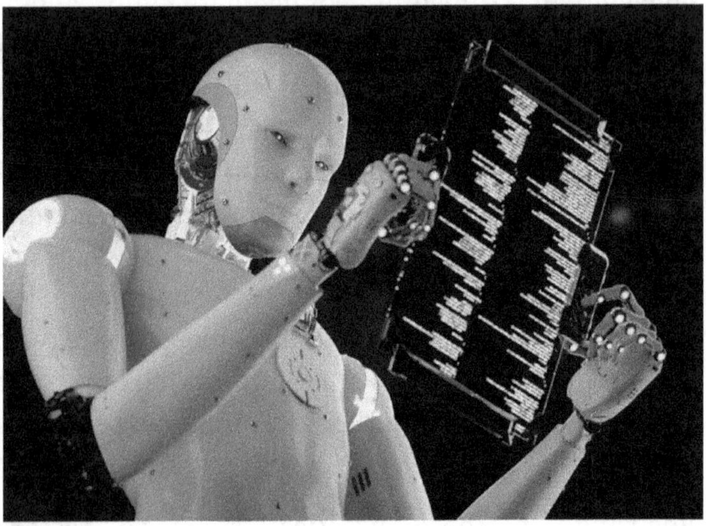

The modern digital environment, marked by constant social media interactions and endless app notifications, surrounds individuals with a never-ending flow of stimuli. This inundation can overwhelm our brain's ability to process dopamine, a crucial neurotransmitter linked to motivation and reward (Firth et al., 2019). Dopamine facilitates focus, serves as a rewarding system for accomplished tasks, and generally fuels our drive to engage with meaningful activities. However, when bombarded consistently by online stimuli, the brain may gradually become less sensitive to dopamine, leading to significant challenges in maintaining focus and clarity.

Engineered for Engagement

Social media platforms engineer their interfaces to maximize engagement by deliberately tapping into our dopamine systems. Notifications on social media offer sporadic rewards, similar to the mechanics behind slot machines. Each like or comment can generate a small release of dopamine, sparking a cycle of immediate gratification and anticipation of future rewards. (George et al., 2024). This process creates a cycle where the brain craves engagement, fostering compulsive behavior. Over time, the need for a "dopamine hit" from digital interactions can lead to anxiety the moment one steps away from these platforms.

The Gaming Factor

Modern gaming adds another layer to this digital dopamine conversation. Video games are designed to provide immediate rewards and lure players into extended sessions. High scores, the thrill of winning, and the endless quest for achievement level-ups keep dopamine levels elevated, making it difficult to resist returning to the game. The mechanic loops of challenges and instant gratification manipulate players into longer playtimes, often at the expense of productive and meaningful offline pursuits. Constant engagement in gaming can distort a person's perception of time and result in neglecting important life responsibilities.

Fragmentation of Attention

A major concern with these digital dopamine spikes is the resulting fragmentation of attention. When the brain toggles incessantly between tasks on social media, the mind fails to settle into a mode that supports deep concentration. Attempting to multitask with social media notifications leads to cognitive overload, impairing one's ability to focus on more significant tasks and retain information effectively. Just as digital distractions can monopolize attention, they simultaneously diminish the brain's ability to engage deeply with any single activity.

The Compulsive Cycle

For instance, you might find yourself mindlessly scrolling through an application, despite knowing that you should concentrate on urgent work. This tendency arises because social media can offer unpredictable rewards—one post might not fetch any engagement while the next could elicit a flood of responses. The inherent unpredictability keeps you hooked in a hope-driven cycle, drawing your time and focus away from pressing matters. This compulsive checking damages your capacity to engage in longer, more contemplative thought processes.

Emotional Impact on Well-Being

Additionally, the emotional rollercoaster triggered by social media engagement impacts your mental well-being. Disjointed scrolling through emotionally charged content may elevate cortisol levels, leading to stress and anxiety (George et al., 2024). Coupled with the fluctuating levels of dopamine due to digital stimulation, you may experience heightened worry or irritability, which can further impair your mental clarity and focus.

The Sleep Factor

Sleep, an essential component of cognitive function, suffers considerably from these addictions. The blue light emitted by mobile devices hampers melatonin production, causing sleep disturbances (George et al., 2024). When coupled with exposure to intense content before bedtime, this creates a cycle in which the brain struggles to disengage, keeping individuals alert when they should be resting. Poor sleep only further exacerbates mental fatigue and reduces an individual's ability to manage stress effectively.

Strategies for Breaking the Cycle

To break this cycle, strategies should focus on reducing digital interactions. For example, users can limit social media notifications or set specific times for checking updates. Creating boundaries that reduce interruptions can help retrain the brain to engage more meaningfully and achieve a healthier balance in dopamine levels. Engaging in offline activities such as reading, exercising, or socializing face-to-face can facilitate a more enriching and balanced life experience, helping to replenish the brain's cognitive resources.

Making Informed Decisions

Understanding that our engagement with these platforms is a product of expert design encourages active decision-making regarding how we interact digitally. By recognizing when you're drawn into a dopamine cycle—whether through gaming or social media—you can reclaim a healthier mental space. Encouraging critical thinking about your media consumption and supporting digital detox practices contributes to this conversation. Mindful consumption of digital media can empower individuals, enhancing mental clarity and promoting better well-being.

Ultimately, the widespread influence of social media, gaming, and notifications highlights the urgent need to assess our relationship with technology. These platforms can provide spaces for connection and recreation, but they should be used mindfully. Acknowledging their capacity to significantly influence mental processes reminds us to create healthier habits and boundaries that foster mental clarity, allowing us to focus on genuinely fulfilling human experiences.

Concluding Thoughts

Have you ever found it challenging to maintain focus, even during activities you enjoy? You may start working on a big project or immerse yourself in a captivating book, but distractions like phone notifications or social media updates frequently divert your attention. This phenomenon can feel like your mind is working against you, making it difficult to concentrate and achieve your long-term goals. This chapter seeks to shed light on what's happening in your brain, particularly the role of dopamine, and how you can regain control over distractions. Understanding these mechanisms can empower you to enhance your focus, discipline, and productivity in pursuing meaningful objectives.

In addition to that, dopamine plays a crucial role in motivation, focus, and discipline, acting as a key component of the brain's reward system. High achievers can benefit significantly from understanding how dopamine drives their behavior and productivity. When you work toward a reward, like completing a project, dopamine levels elevate, enhancing your motivation and drive. However, maintaining a healthy dopamine balance is essential. Too much dopamine can lead to impulsivity, pulling your focus toward immediate gratification rather than the long-term goals that require discipline. Recognizing the influence of dopamine on your behavior allows you to align your habits with success and improve your ability to concentrate amidst a world filled with distractions.

But what happens when these strategies alone are not enough to truly disengage from the cycle of overstimulation, fatigue, and anxiety? What deeper truth lies beneath the surface of this dopamine crash, revealing connections that could fundamentally change your relationship with your own mind? The revelations ahead may shed light on the profound ways overstimulation can lead to burnout, challenging you to rethink how you approach both your work and leisure. The journey to reclaiming your focus and mental clarity is just beginning—stay tuned!

Chapter 3: The Dopamine Crash: How Overstimulation Leads to Fatigue, Anxiety, and Burnout

The rush of a social media notification or the thrill of reaching a new level in a video game can quickly overshadow everything else, making it feel dull by comparison. Tasks that once brought joy or satisfaction now often appear as mundane chores. Focusing on work becomes harder than ever after a session of high-speed scrolling through posts or engaging in games. Many people encounter this strange phenomenon where our brains crave more of those dopamine-inducing activities that offer immediate gratification, leaving us trapped in a cycle where real-world responsibilities feel overwhelming or insignificant.

You might ask yourself, Why does this happen? How is it that activities once enjoyable have lost their sparkle, replaced by an overpowering urge for next-level stimuli? This chapter addresses these questions, examining how excessive dopamine stimulation alters our brain's reward system, resulting in fatigue and anxiety, which in turn impact our motivation and productivity. As we reveal the profound implications of this overstimulation, you'll gain insights into restoring balance in a world crafted to keep you engaged.

Why Motivation Disappears When You Flood Your Brain With Dopamine

The Impact of Excessive Dopamine

When dopamine levels in the brain get excessively stimulated, your motivation takes a hit. This neurotransmitter is crucial for why you feel excited about certain activities, and when there's too much of it, your brain starts getting numb, creating a domino effect on how you pursue and enjoy activities that once seemed delightful. These activities, which formerly captivated your interest, begin to lose their appeal.

This desensitization largely stems from the quick-hit satisfaction that activities like social media scrolling or video gaming provide. Just like having too much sugar dulls your taste buds over time, continuous dopamine overload from these high-stimulation activities alters your brain chemistry, making tasks that require more patience and perseverance feel mundane and less rewarding.

Understanding Dopamine Overload

Let's talk about dopamine overload and how it works in your brain. Your neural system wasn't designed to handle constant high-level dopamine bombardments without consequences. This neurotransmitter plays a vital role in helping you remember what feels good, so when you experience huge bursts of it, your brain becomes less sensitive to its presence. Tasks you were once eager to complete start feeling uninspiring. It's like listening to your favorite song on repeat until it loses its magic.

Indulging in high-stimulation activities provides immediate gratification, making it hard to find pleasure in activities that require prolonged effort. For instance, picking up a book suddenly seems daunting compared to the easy thrill of an online game. Your brain gets overly accustomed to these dopamine jolts, and as a result, long-term goals become overshadowed by the allure of immediate rewards that do not demand much effort or time investment.

The Cycle of Instant Gratification

In this cycle of instant gratification, you may notice significant changes in your behavioral patterns. You might begin to prioritize activities that provide quick dopamine boosts over essential habits that build long-term success. For example, instead of investing time in skill development or exercise, you might devote more time to the quick dopamine fixes offered by social media and video games. Imagine being a student who can hardly find the motivation to study because scrolling through endless videos seems far more tempting than tackling textbooks. A cycle of abandoning productive pursuits for more immediately gratifying ones sets in, causing you to inadvertently sidestep meaningful engagement and achievement.

The Psychological Aftermath

The psychological aftermath of this overstimulation is glaring in its impact on your daily life and motivation. Everyday responsibilities like work or home chores become unbearable, morphing into Herculean tasks. Previously engaging duties transform into dreary obligations, and the desire to avoid this tedium drags many into a loop of procrastination and delay. The satisfaction that should come from completing tasks feels conspicuously absent. Life's richness seems diminished as your motivation to engage deeply in activities decreases. For instance, someone whose daily experience is filled with constant dopamine surges from gaming may find work hours painfully dull. The excitement that should accompany the achievement of something significant fades, casting a shadow of dissatisfaction over daily life.

The Widening Gap of Ambition

Through intense stimulation, you often unknowingly drift away from activities that require more effort and offer intrinsic long-term rewards. This divergence results in a widening gap between your current state and your potential. Over time, you may become trapped, yearning for more intense stimulation to feel anything at all, while everyday tasks drag down your mood and drive. Picture a person who once enjoyed gardening now dreading time spent with plants because nothing compares to the thrill of an online duel. The consequences can be profound, leading to frustration and a pervasive sense of unfulfillment that undermines your self-esteem. This results in a feeling of constant unrest, where only a heightened awareness of the cycle's harshness can ignite the desire for change.

The Need for Cognitive Awareness

Understanding the negative effects of excessive dopamine exposure is key to examining its origins and formulating alternative engagement strategies. Cognitive awareness comes alive when you observe your personal habits and their links to pleasure and reward. Recognizing how dopamine creates a false sense of satisfaction can help you understand the genuine effects of continuous overstimulation on your mental health and motivation. As the craving for activities that offer immediate rewards grows, the loss of motivation becomes a common outcome, leading to more nuanced discussions about breaking free from the cycle of excess. Your brain resists being deprived of regular dopamine rewards, creating a complicated scenario as you manage tasks, plan, and take action.

Understanding Dopamine Withdrawal

The happy feelings you get from dopamine highs can lead to feelings of withdrawal later. Looking at the link between clinical depression symptoms and dopamine withdrawal helps us understand these issues better. This allows you to regain your balance and motivation while pursuing meaningful goals that are connected to the quiet moments in life, helping your mind grow and find true satisfaction.

How Dopamine Withdrawal Mimics Depression

The Withdrawal Experience

Stepping away from the constant flood of dopamine-boosting distractions is like suddenly stopping a habit you love but know isn't good for you, like munching on sugary snacks. The chronic intake of dopamine rewards—from social media likes to video game victories—has already trained our minds to crave immediate gratification. This preference slowly undermines motivation and prioritizes short-lived pleasures over long-term goals. As we attempt to cut back or abstain from these activities, the withdrawal symptoms can eerily mimic symptoms of clinical depression.

The Lethargy of Detox

Imagine this: you return home after a long day at work and forgo your usual screen time. Instead of feeling relaxed, you're overcome by a sense of lethargy and emptiness. Usually, moments like these stand out compared to the lively digital interactions you often take part in. This fatigue isn't just physical; it tugs at your very mental fiber, leading to an absence of relatability with routines once treasured. These symptoms stem from a brain struggling to adjust to a lower level of dopamine stimulation.

Neurological Impacts of Reduced Dopamine

From a neurological perspective, moving to a lower dopamine environment is like taking away a key support from a strong arch. Our brains, heavily reliant on dopamine for regulating pleasure and motivation, struggle to maintain balance without it. The mood swings you experience aren't just temporary annoyances; they're part of a larger cycle of symptoms that increase anxiety and create a lasting feeling of dissatisfaction. Your brain, used to getting pleasure from high-dopamine activities, now faces a lack of stimulation, which leads it to send out distress signals that you feel as moodiness and restlessness (Gupta et al., 2020).

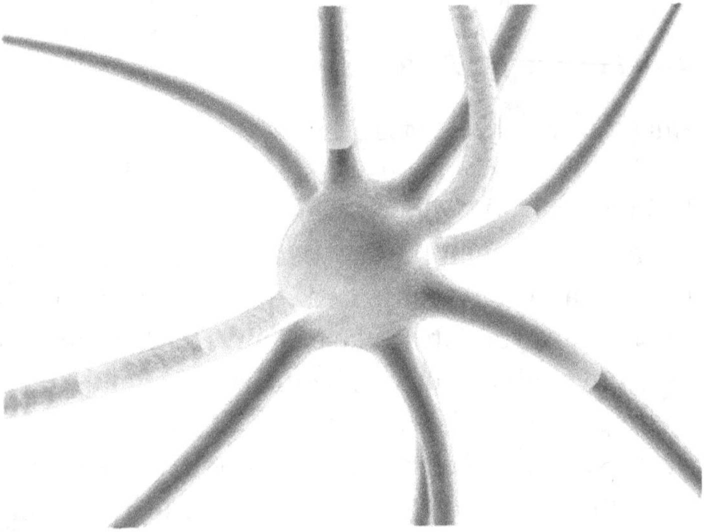

The Cycle of Emotional Instability

As this low-dopamine pattern persists, we might find ourselves caught in a cycle of emotional instability. One day, you might feel unusually irritable, snapping at loved one's over minor issues. The next day, you battle a fog that clutters your thoughts, making even simple tasks insurmountable. This emotional up-and-down is strongly connected to routines lacking in dopamine, highlighting the important relationship between neurotransmitter balance and mental stability. The feeling of frustration when enjoyable tasks no longer excite you, replaced by indifference, shows the unstable reward pathways in your brain (nadiahall5, 2024).

The Digital Detox Dilemma

In our effort to understand these changes, let's look at the typical situation of someone starting a digital detox. Such a person may initially revel in newfound time, perhaps dedicating it to long-forgotten hobbies. But soon, the withdrawal kicks in. Mornings, once started with caffeine boosts and social media scrolling, now feel empty and dragging.

Withdrawal symptoms feel like the tiredness of a hangover, gradually turning any initial excitement into a general feeling of boredom.

Redefining Interaction With the World

Recognizing this pattern can be life-changing. Dealing with dopamine withdrawal begins with recognizing the limited behaviors that used to bring you a lot of pleasure. Instead of getting frustrated about losing productivity or happiness, you can see these experiences as a chance to rethink how you interact with the world around you. This may involve slowly appreciating activities that promote a lower, steadier, but ultimately more satisfying level of dopamine stimulation. Perhaps a morning spent gardening or an evening walk can offer pleasures often drowned out by louder stimuli.

The Impact on Focus and Productivity

Withdrawal symptoms not only affect mood but also impact focus and clarity. As dopamine levels plunge, productivity can stumble. Tasks requiring sustained attention turn daunting, causing frequent procrastination. If unchecked, this domino effect leaves cognitive functions ravaged. Such states necessitate interventions designed to foster equilibrium, much like transitioning from feast to balanced meals. Slowly, as dopamine pathways recalibrate, cognitive faculties and mood can regain balance, enabling more authentic interactions and promoting lasting well-being.

The Power of Small Changes

Starting with small changes can create a ripple effect. Say you're accustomed to checking your phone the first thing in the morning—substitute that burst of dopamine with a brief stretch or meditation. While it may feel unrewarding initially, practicing such habits can incrementally bolster resilience. Each choice to distance oneself from excessive dopamine lifts a little of the fog, reestablishing deeper connections within previously neglected parts of the self.

Addressing Procrastination and Fatigue

Having strapped ourselves tightly to dopamine's highs and lows, it's no surprise that overstimulation pushes us further into the shadows of mental fatigue. This fatigue is insidious—it clouds judgment, stifles ambition, and weaves procrastination into the fabric of daily life. Proactively addressing these challenges involves using strategies that positively and sustainably reengage your dopamine pathways.

As we explore ways to address cognitive issues and reduced productivity, it becomes clear that our relationship with dopamine involves finding balance. Choosing to leave behind extreme highs in favor of more thoughtful and controlled lows is not only helpful but also vital for building a life filled with satisfaction and stability. Tackling overstimulation allows us to rediscover the beauty of balance, creating a story where mental health stands against chaotic overindulgence.

The Trap of Procrastination, Brain Fog, and Mental Exhaustion

The Link Between Dopamine Withdrawal and Procrastination

The previous section explored the concept of dopamine withdrawal, shedding light on how it mirrors the symptoms of depression. Now, let's move on to the practical challenges that come up when overstimulation causes procrastination and mental stagnation. This inevitable sequence reflects the harsh realities faced in everyday life when dopamine levels fluctuate drastically. There is an important connection between the emotional effects of dopamine depletion and the real productivity challenges we're discussing here. These shifts happen naturally; when dopamine levels drop, our thinking doesn't just slow down—it gets stuck in confusion and indecision.

While dopamine drives motivation and reward, its overproduction can lead to ongoing mental fatigue and a decreased ability to meet demands. Now we can see the broader impacts of dopamine overindulgence on daily life.

The Impact of High-Dopamine Stimuli

Constant exposure to high-dopamine stimuli significantly impacts cognitive performance, resulting in what many refer to as brain fog. For example, consider the widespread use of smartphones. What might start as a simple swipe quickly morphs into hours lost in digital engagement, impairing one's ability to focus on present tasks or make clear decisions. This distraction isn't just confined to personal life; it extends into work and school, where the constant demand to stay updated leads to shorter attention spans and slower information processing.

Procrastination as a Defense Mechanism

Procrastination often arises as a natural reaction to this mental overload, serving as a defense against overwhelming demands. Picture a student or employee, swamped by notifications that demand their attention. The idea of starting a project becomes daunting, not because of the project's complexity, but due to an inability to mentally disconnect from the oversaturated stimulus environment. Such scenarios illuminate how procrastination offers temporary relief, albeit interspersed with guilt for neglected duties. This guilt, in turn, cyclically nudges anxiety levels upward, draining further motivation and exacerbating the problem. One quickly finds themselves ensnared in a confounding loop of intent, delayed execution, regret, and rising anxiety—a typical manifestation of ADHD paralysis where tasks rather than threats feed the defense mechanism (Breeze Well-Being, 2024).

Structured Solutions for Mental Fog

To fight the negative effects of too much stimulation and the problems it creates for our thinking, it's important to use clear and organized methods.

Setting specific and achievable goals helps clear up mental confusion by giving us a clear path to follow. Dividing tasks into smaller, more manageable parts makes them feel less overwhelming, similar to tips often recommended for beating procrastination.

For example, the technique of time blocking involves setting aside certain times to work on specific tasks, which helps create a routine that includes breaks and prevents feeling stuck (Breeze Well-Being, 2024). This method offers a concrete sense of progression, countering the inertia of constant mental bombardment.

Finding Balance in an Overstimulated World

The pursuit of productivity in an overstimulated age equates to finding balance in an environment where constant alerts and updates compete for our attention. Crafting routines that promote mindfulness, taking deliberate breaks, and cultivating hobbies detached from screens can ameliorate the mental exhaustion stemming from overstimulation. While these approaches demand conscious effort, they can guide users towards a more engaged and fulfilling manner of processing their tasks and achieving their goals.

Summary and Reflections

The quick thrill from social media notifications or advancing levels in video games often overshadows meaningful activities, making them feel dull by comparison. Once-enjoyable tasks can become mundane chores, leading to a strange craving for dopamine-driven activities that provide immediate gratification. This chapter explores the reasons behind this phenomenon, highlighting how excessive dopamine stimulation alters our brain's reward system. This overstimulation can result in feelings of fatigue and anxiety, which ultimately impact our motivation and productivity. Understanding the implications of this phenomenon can help us regain balance in our increasingly engaging world.

On top of that, excessive stimulation of dopamine can dull your motivation and desensitize your brain to activities that once brought joy. Just as consuming too much sugar can numb your taste buds, an overload of high-stimulation activities can change your brain chemistry, making it difficult to enjoy tasks that require patience and perseverance. This creates a cycle of instant gratification, where you prioritize quick hits of pleasure over essential habits and long-term success. As a result, responsibilities feel daunting, leading to procrastination and a sense of unfulfillment, culminating in a widening gap between your current state and your potential.

Lastly, to combat the negative effects of excessive dopamine exposure, developing cognitive awareness is crucial. Recognizing the impact of overstimulation on mental health and motivation can empower you to create alternative engagement strategies. Starting a digital detox may lead to withdrawal symptoms that mirror depression, highlighting the importance of finding balance. However, what if these challenges run deeper than mere willpower? What if the path to restoring your motivation isn't just about minimizing distractions, but instead involves a profound transformation of how you engage with the world around you?

As we transition into the next chapter, prepare to explore the Dopamine Detox Blueprint—a comprehensive plan designed to reset your brain in just 7 or 14 days. This blueprint holds the key to reclaiming your focus, revitalizing your motivation, and paving the way for lasting fulfillment. The revelations and strategies ahead might forever change your approach to dopamine, and your relationship with pleasure and productivity may never be the same.

Chapter 4: The Dopamine Detox Blueprint: How to Reset Your Brain in 7 or 14 Days

In a world full of distractions vying for our attention, a dopamine detox can be a great solution. Think of it as hitting the reset button on your mind, clearing out the extra noise to help you see things more clearly and focus better. This detox isn't just a quick break; it's a journey that helps you take back your mental clarity and regain control over your habits.

This chapter provides a comprehensive guide for implementing a dopamine detox—a methodical approach to regaining your focus and minimizing the overwhelming distractions that have become prevalent. Whether it's identifying when distractions are at their highest or discovering new strategies to bring calm into your daily routine, these steps are intended to help you change how you engage with your surroundings and improve your ability to concentrate on what really matters.

Choosing Your Detox Level: Light, Standard, or Hard Mode

Tailoring your detox level to fit your lifestyle and patterns of overstimulation is essential for sustainable change and an effective mental reset.

Gradual change serves as your roadmap, facilitating a smoother detox journey.

Each level offers a customizable approach based on your digital engagement and overstimulation. Think of it as a toolkit where each option addresses different needs, from minor adjustments to significant lifestyle changes designed to improve mental clarity.

	Description
Light mode	A Gentle start: Perfect for those new to dopamine detox or experiencing moderate stimulation. It focuses on manageable changes like reducing screen time in the evenings. Simple adjustments, such as swapping your phone for a book before bed, provide a gentle introduction to less stimulating habits.
Standard mode	Cultivating a routine: Suited for those frequently encountering overstimulation. This level promotes consistent routines that help declutter the mind. When you reduce multitasking and dedicate specific time blocks for focused work, you can

	improve overall productivity and build enduring habits.
Hard mode	Breaking free: For individuals facing severe digital overload, hard mode offers a more intensive approach. It requires a strong commitment to disconnect from screens for extended periods and reassess daily habits. Strategies might include whole weekends without technology or creating tech-free zones to foster deeper focus and mental recalibration.

Selecting the right detox level is a strategic decision that balances personal needs and boundaries while promoting mental clarity. A personalized approach increases chances of long-term success, empowering you to manage your digital habits effectively. This journey becomes meaningful, leading to greater equilibrium in everyday life.

The chosen detox level shapes your detox journey, similar to starting a fitness regimen. Be prepared for withdrawal symptoms, unease, or newfound mental space—each signifies progress as you adapt to your new habits (Setia et al., 2025).

7-Day Dopamine Detox Blueprint

The 7-Day Dopamine Detox Blueprint is designed to help you reset your brain and regain focus amidst constant digital distractions. Over the course of the week, you'll assess your daily habits, make gradual changes to reduce overstimulation, and introduce healthier practices that foster mindfulness and creativity.

	Goal	Activity	Challenge/ reflection
Day 1	**Acknowle-ging the chaos**	Start by tracking your daily activities to identify when you feel most distracted or overstimulated. Note how much time you spend on social media, checking emails, or mindlessly watching TV.	Recognizing these patterns is the first step to understanding what pulls your attention away from important tasks.
Day 2	**Make gradual changes**	Begin reducing overstimulation gradually.	If you usually check social media first

		Silence notifications on your phone and laptop to limit distractions.	thing in the morning, set limits on your screen time during the day.
Day 3	**Transition to healthier habits**	Incorporate mindfulness practices into your routine. Try meditation or deep breathing to enhance focus and mental clarity.	These practices can improve brain health and help manage stress.
Day 4	**Engage in creative outlets**	Replace screen time with creative pursuits like drawing, writing, or playing a musical instrument.	Use these activities to refocus your mind and channel your energy constructivel y.

Day 5	**Set boundaries with devices**	Define specific times for checking emails and social media. Create tech-free zones, such as during meals or an hour before bed.	This intentional engagement helps you gain greater control over your screen time.
Day 6	**Introduce breaks**	Use the Pomodoro Technique—work for 25 minutes, then take a 5-minute break. Use these breaks to stretch, grab a snack, or take a brief walk.	Regular breaks help reduce overstimulation while promoting sustained focus.
Day 7	**Reclaim your cognitive space**	Review your progress from the week. Assess what habits have changed and how you feel about your focus and productivity.	Remember, this detox isn't about eliminating dopamine activities but reclaiming your cognitive space for better mental clarity and well-being.

A Comprehensive Guide to Practicing Meditation Step by Step

Meditation is a powerful practice that offers numerous benefits for the mind and body, helping to cultivate inner peace and clarity. This guide will take you through the steps necessary to begin your meditation journey, providing you with the tools and techniques to enhance your experience and deepen your practice.

- **Find a quiet space:** Choose a calm and quiet place where you won't be disturbed. It could be a cozy corner of your home or a peaceful outdoor spot.
- **Get comfortable:** Sit or lie down in a comfortable position. You can sit cross-legged on the floor, on a cushion, or in a chair with your feet flat on the ground. Keep your back straight to allow for deep breathing.
- **Close your eyes:** Gently close your eyes to minimize distractions and turn your focus inward.
- **Take deep breaths:** Start with a few deep breaths. Inhale deeply through your nose, filling your lungs, and exhale slowly through your mouth. Repeat this a few times to relax.

- **Focus on your breath:** Shift your attention to your breath. Notice the sensations of inhaling and exhaling. If your mind wanders, gently bring your focus back to your breath without judgment.
- **Set a timer:** Decide how long you want to meditate. Set a timer for your desired duration (5 to 10 minutes is a good start for beginners).
- **Gradually end the session:** When the timer goes off, take a few deep breaths and slowly bring your awareness back to your surroundings. Open your eyes when you're ready and take a moment to notice how you feel.

Easy Techniques for Practicing Deep Breathing

Deep breathing is a simple yet effective technique that can help alleviate stress, promote relaxation, and enhance overall well-being. As you follow these easy steps to practice deep breathing, you can cultivate a sense of calm and clarity in your daily life.

- **Find a comfortable position:** Sit or lie down in a comfortable position. Make sure your body is relaxed and supported.

- **Place your hands:** Rest one hand on your chest and the other on your belly. This will help you feel your breath.
- **Inhale deeply:** Breathe in slowly through your nose for a count of four. Feel your belly rise as you fill your lungs with air.
- **Hold your breath**: Hold your breath for a count of four, keeping your body relaxed.
- **Exhale slowly:** Exhale slowly through your mouth for a count of six, feeling your belly fall. Focus on releasing any tension or stress.
- **Repeat the cycle:** Continue this cycle of deep breathing for 5 to 10 minutes. Aim to inhale for four counts, hold for four counts, and exhale for six counts.
- **Gradually return to normal breathing:** After your session, allow your breath to return to its natural rhythm. Take a moment to notice how you feel.

14-Day Dopamine Detox Blueprint

This two-week program allows you to deeply explore your digital habits, pinpoint the triggers that cause overstimulation, and make gradual changes that promote healthier routines. Choosing this 14-day detox instead of a shorter version is beneficial to establish lasting habits, engage in fulfilling activities, and recognize your achievements, ultimately paving the way for ongoing personal growth and increased productivity.

Week 1: Building Awareness and Initial Changes

	Goal	Activity	Reflection/challenge
Day 1	**Acknowledge your digital environment**	Reflect on your current digital habits. Write down the main distractions in your life, such as social media, emails, or games, and how they affect your daily productivity and mood.	Understanding your digital landscape is crucial for initiating change.
Day 2	**Identify specific triggers**	Keep a log of when you feel compelled to check your devices. Note the time, place, and emotions that	Uncover patterns in your triggers, which are important for forming your detox strategy.

		prompt this behavior.	
Day 3	**Set detox goals**	Define clear and specific goals for your dopamine detox. Decide what you want to achieve in the next two weeks, such as reducing screen time or engaging in more offline activities.	Writing down your goals increases accountability and motivation.
Day 4	**Start with small reductions**	Begin reducing your exposure to digital distractions. Silence non-essential notifications and limit mindless scrolling by setting specific times for social media use, such as 30 minutes at lunch.	Small, manageable changes can lead to sustainable habits.

Day 5	**Create a more focused workspace**	Redesign your workspace to minimize distractions. Clear away unnecessary items and organize your environment to promote focus. Consider a dedicated workspace free from technology during your detox.	A tidy workspace can enhance mental clarity and productivity.
Day 6	**Incorporate mindfulness practices**	Introduce mindfulness techniques such as daily meditation or breathwork. Allocate 5-10 minutes each day to practice, enhancing your ability to manage distractions and maintain focus.	Mindfulness nurtures mental resilience and aids in recognizing urges for instant gratification.

Day 7	**Engage in offline activities**	Dedicate time to non-digital pursuits. Choose hobbies that require active engagement, such as cooking, exercising, or reading. This helps divert attention from screens and enriches your life.	Engaging in offline activities can create a satisfying alternative to digital distractions.

Week 2: Strengthening Resilience and Maintaining Progress

	Goal	**Activity**	**Reflection/challenge**
Day 8	**Regularly review progress**	At the end of the week, assess your achievements and challenges. What strategies worked well? Where did you struggle?	Reflecting on your progress helps reinforce successes and adjust behaviors.
Day 9	**Introduce structured breaks**	Adopt the Pomodoro Technique to manage work	Regular breaks help maintain energy levels and cognitive

		sessions. Work for 25 minutes and take a 5-minute break. Use breaks for stretching or walking to recharge your mind.	focus throughout the day.
Day 10	**Emphasize healthy nutrition**	Focus on nutrition that supports mental clarity. Prepare balanced meals with whole foods, such as lean proteins, whole grains, and plenty of fruits and vegetables.	Good nutrition fuels your brain, helping you fight off cravings for quick dopamine hits.
Day 11	**Set boundaries for technology use**	Establish clear bounadaries for using devices. For example, designate specific times for checking emails or social media, and keep screens out of bedrooms or during meals.	Setting boundaries helps you regain control over your devices and reduce compulsive behavior.

Day 12	**Create social accountability**	Share your detox journey with friends or family members. Seek a support buddy who can join you in reducing distractions and achieving goals.	Having a support system can motivate you to stay committed and accountable.
Day 13	**Plan post-detox**	Draft a plan for sustaining the healthy habits you've formed during the detox. Identify what you want to maintain in your daily routine moving forward.	Forward planning helps ensure the positive changes stick, reinforcing long-term growth.
Day 14	**Create social accountability**	Reflect on the past two weeks, celebrating your achievements and the changes you've made in your focus and productivity.	Treat yourself to something enjoyable (not technology-related) as a reward for your hard work and commitment to personal growth.

Following this 14-day dopamine detox blueprint allows you to reset your brain and establish healthier habits that enhance focus and productivity. The journey emphasizes awareness, gradual changes, and resilience, guiding you toward a more balanced relationship with technology.

What to Expect in the First 24-48 Hours

A New Journey Begins

Stepping into the first phase of a dopamine detox can feel like embarking on a new journey, where the first few days present the most palpable changes and hurdles. You're likely to notice heightened awareness and cravings as your brain begins adjusting to reduced stimuli. These early challenges are a temporary yet critical part of resetting your mental state and can offer valuable insights into your habits and distractions. The choice of a detox strategy, be it a full abstention from digital devices or a more moderate reduction in screen time, significantly impacts your experience during this phase.

Anticipating Withdrawal Symptoms

When starting this detox, be prepared for withdrawal symptoms to emerge. According to research, these symptoms can manifest as irritability, restlessness, or even anxiety (Gould,

2010). Such feelings reflect the brain's response to a shift in dopamine levels that often results from stimulus overexposure. It's akin to the discomfort experienced during substance withdrawal, as the brain's reward system, particularly the nucleus accumbens, recalibrates (Goldstein & Volkow, 2011). While these feelings may be uncomfortable, understanding their temporary nature is key. They signify that the detox process is working, indicating the neural pathways' gradual return to their natural state.

Seizing the Opportunity for Self-Reflection

The moment you notice these cravings and heightened awareness, take it as an opportunity for self-reflection. Recognizing these sensations can help identify how stimulants have shaped your daily life. Imagine this as a pause button, allowing a deeper understanding of your reliance on instant gratification. Journaling can be an effective tool here. By putting thoughts on paper, you can track progress and pinpoint specific situations that trigger cravings. This practice is not just a record-keeping exercise but a space where personal evolution unfolds.

Starting Your Journaling Practice

Begin the journaling process by dedicating 10-15 minutes each morning or evening to writing. Start with simple prompts such as, “What cravings did I notice today?” or “How did I feel without my usual stimuli?” Over time, extend this practice to include reflections on how you navigated these feelings. These entries, over weeks, could reveal patterns that might otherwise go unnoticed.

Final Insights

Many individuals find themselves absorbed in the endless scroll of social media, losing track of time as minutes turn into hours. This constant checking of emails and notifications leads to a chaotic mental state where distractions dominate, leaving people feeling unproductive and mentally scattered. If this resonates with you, know you're not alone. In our always-on world, focusing can feel impossible. However, regaining control over your attention is achievable, starting with recognizing patterns of overstimulation. This chapter outlines a comprehensive guide to implementing a dopamine detox, offering strategies to minimize distractions and improve concentration on what truly matters.

The 7-Day Dopamine Detox Blueprint provides a structured approach to resetting your brain. Each day emphasizes different activities aimed at reducing overstimulation and fostering healthier habits. On Day 1, acknowledge your current habits by tracking distractions, which is essential for understanding what pulls your focus. On Day 2, begin silencing notifications to gradually reduce interruptions. By Day 3, incorporate practices like meditation to enhance your mental clarity. The plan progresses through creative outlets on Day 4, setting boundaries with devices on Day 5, and using techniques like the Pomodoro Technique on Day 6. The final day focuses on reflecting on your progress and committing to mindful engagement, ensuring long-term benefits beyond the detox period.

For those seeking a deeper exploration, the 14-Day Dopamine Detox Blueprint allows for more comprehensive adjustments to your digital habits. In Week 1, build awareness by reflecting on your digital environment and identifying triggers for distraction. This week includes creating a focused workspace and introducing mindfulness practices. Week 2 emphasizes maintaining progress by incorporating structured breaks, maintaining healthy nutrition, and setting boundaries with technology. This two-week challenge aims to help develop lasting habits and celebrates your achievements, paving the way for ongoing personal growth and enriched productivity.

But what happens once you've completed the detox? How do you ensure that you don't slip back into the old patterns of digital addiction that once held you captive? The next chapter will delve into the psychological strategies and mindset shifts crucial for not only maintaining the progress you've made but also for establishing a new relationship with technology that enhances your life rather than detracts from it. Are you ready to break free from the chains of digital dependence and reclaim your mental clarity? The journey continues—stay tuned!

Chapter 5: The Mental Reset: Breaking Free From Digital Addiction

Have you ever caught yourself reaching for your phone without even thinking, only to snap back to reality a few minutes later, wondering where the time went? You're not alone. In today's hyper-connected world, digital devices have become such an integral part of our lives that breaking free from their grasp seems almost impossible. But consider what it would be like to regain control over your time and attention.

Imagine implementing strategies that help you consciously reduce distractions and reclaim moments of genuine focus. This chapter explores ways to slowly cut down on digital distractions using proven methods. By making small but effective changes to your daily routine, you'll develop a healthier relationship with technology, resulting in improved productivity and clearer thinking.

Strategies for Gradual Reduction of Digital Distractions

Embracing a Sustainable Approach

Diving headfirst into the abyss of digital detox can seem overwhelming. It's like deciding to sprint a marathon without warming up; total cessation often feels too drastic, ineffective, and, frankly, counterproductive. Gradually phasing digital reliance out of our daily routine, however, presents a far more sustainable path. Just think of modest shifts as the stepping stones across the wide river of change.

Setting Specific Times for Social Media Use

Begin by setting specific times for social media use, creating a symbiotic relationship with technology rather than a parasitic one. Assigning fixed time slots for social engagement noticeably minimizes impulse checking, establishing a routine that brings order and mindfulness.

- Decide on set times during the day or week when you'll allow yourself to check social platforms. Morning, lunch, or post-work wind down are popular choices.

- Mark these chosen times in your calendar or planner as "social media time," turning what could be chaotic into a concrete, integral part of the day.

- Utilize silent reminders—be it phone alarms, sticky notes on your workspace, or entries in a digital planner—to keep you committed and present during these moments.

Taking Control of Notifications

Notifications act like the siren's call, constantly tugging at our attention. When you control these alerts, you regain command over your focus. With fewer interruptions, productivity thrives, stress decreases, and life feels less reactive and more proactive.

- Identify which of your apps frequently interrupt your day with notifications. Are they truly necessary, or just indulgent distractions?

- Disable alerts from those apps that have little to no bearing on your daily priorities. You'll be amazed at how much headspace you recover.

- Allocate brief intervals specifically for checking these notifications, as they may be optional but are still somewhat important. Perhaps once mid-morning, once after lunch, and once early evening.

Filtering Your News Consumption

In a world filled with many voices competing for attention, it's important to tune out the noise and select trustworthy sources that help improve your mental clarity.

- Compile a roster of reputable, unbiased news sources through research and recommendations. These outlets should promise not just headline buzz but comprehensive reporting.
- Subscribe to or follow only these vetted channels, and avoid getting pulled into rabbit holes of sensationalism.
- Define a rhythm for news consumption—maybe a quick scan in the morning and a debrief in the evening, steering clear of around-the-clock news cycles that drain emotional energy.

Real-Life Success Story

Imagine a young entrepreneur who experienced a dramatic boost in productivity after implementing these thoughtful strategies. Recognizing the chaos of constant notifications and endless scrolling, she decided to carve out her morning commute as dedicated social media time. Instead of mindlessly scrolling throughout the day, she used this specific time to catch up on her social networks and connect with her online community.

To further enhance her focus, she switched off all but essential work-related alerts, allowing her to create a distraction-free environment during her core working hours. By eliminating unnecessary interruptions, she found that she could dive deeper into her tasks and maintain a higher level of concentration.

Additionally, she embraced a twice-daily check-in for the news, allowing her to stay informed without becoming overwhelmed. With this structured approach, she could control when and how she consumed information, which greatly reduced anxiety about missing out on important updates.

This small but mighty shift in her routine granted her grounded mornings where she could mentally prepare for the day ahead. It also provided uninterrupted work hours, enabling her to accomplish more in less time. The result was a significant decrease in her anxiety levels, as she felt confident about staying "in the know" without the constant pressure of information overload. Overall, these intentional changes allowed her to thrive both personally and professionally.

Building on Small Changes

These changes are easier to integrate into your lifestyle compared to a cold-turkey shutdown. Plus, you're likely to see improvements not only in focus and peace of mind, but also in work performance and leisure satisfaction. Splitting a dense task into ultra-digestible, meaningful sections makes climbing mountains out of molehills both rewarding and manageable.

Look ahead, because in the next part of this chapter, you'll uncover more methods to reduce phone addiction. The innovative "Gray Screen" technique awaits, offering advanced options designed to hack our compulsive habits. As you engage with these tools, remember that even ambitious goals like crafting more intentional relationships with our devices unfold best when tackled in stride.

Implementing the "Gray Screen" Method

The Power of Grayscale

The grayscale method can appear deceptively simple, yet it's an ingenious hack for reducing phone usage. Bright and vibrant colors often captivate our attention. They stimulate our brains, encouraging us to keep interacting with our devices. The grayscale trick exploits the basic psychological principle of reducing these stimuli, thus making phone screens less appealing (Nield, 2019).

Managing Your Environment

Taking charge of our surroundings is key to fighting digital addiction. By making spaces that limit distractions, people can get back their focus and clear thinking. Digital devices constantly feed us information, often resulting in fragmented attention and diminished productivity. Setting up environments that limit these distractions aids in achieving a mental state conducive to deep work and relaxation.

Crafting Focused Work Sessions

One effective way is to set specific times each day for focused work without digital distractions. Dedicating an hour each morning to a task, such as creative writing or brainstorming leads to significant progress with minimal interference. Without constant notifications or the lure of social media, the productivity boost is tangible. These uninterrupted sessions pave the way for higher-quality work output and a more relaxed state of mind post-activity.

Creating a Distraction-Free Workspace

Another essential strategy involves crafting a physical workspace that encourages focus and limits digital influences. Convert a part of your home into a distraction-free zone, primarily for work and creativity. The presence of physical books, whiteboards, and planning journals helps establish an area where concentration can thrive. With little interference from digital devices, this setting encourages true engagement with the task, boosting creativity and performance. These spaces also help people shift into work or creative mode more easily, lessening procrastination and resistance.

Embracing Non-Digital Leisure Activities

Getting involved in non-digital leisure activities is essential for decreasing overstimulation from digital devices. When we pivot to options like reading physical books, solving complex puzzles, or indulging in outdoor sports, we stimulate our minds differently. These activities challenge our creativity while providing an escape from the monotonous digital world. Especially when placed alongside the benefits of a well-curated workspace and scheduled focus time, they form a holistic approach to combating digital addiction.

Cultivating a Balanced Lifestyle

Learning to love these analog activities supports a more balanced lifestyle. Outdoor activities, for instance, not only promote physical health but also afford a sense of freedom and connection to the world. Time spent outdoors refreshes the mind, offering a new perspective that can be invigorating and calming.

Redefining the Digital Relationship

When you pay attention to these non-digital spaces and times, you not only fight digital addiction but also create a way to exist outside the online world. This active management of your environment leads to better concentration, a stronger appreciation for the tasks you do, and, in the end, a new understanding of technology. These changes can inspire greater creativity and a richer, more balanced life experience.

The Transformative Journey

An especially important factor is realizing how these changes open the door to more varied leisure activities and greater self-involvement. The satisfaction derived from a new hiking trail, a compelling book, or a jigsaw puzzle is both rewarding and mentally liberating. Acting as a counterbalance, these activities complement the focus achieved through planned work times and dedicated spaces for creativity and productivity.

Preparing for Further Strategies

The next part of this chapter will explore how to diversify leisure activities. As we expand our range of screen-free hobbies, we cultivate a rich lifestyle that goes beyond digital distractions. As we expand our repertoire of screen-free hobbies, we nurture a fulfilling lifestyle that transcends digital distractions.

In summary, building environments that avoid digital overstimulation requires careful choices about how and when we use technology. As you schedule time for focused work, design physical spaces that minimize digital distractions, and engage in non-digital activities, we actively pave the way for mental clarity and relaxation. These strategies not only improve productivity and creativity but also promote a healthier mindset and a greater appreciation for the world beyond our screens. They help lighten the mental load of digital noise, allowing us to take back control of our lives and goals.

Establishing Dopamine-Free Zones

Once we remove the overwhelming appeal of our screens, the next important step is to adjust the physical spaces around us.

Designating Focused Work Times

Start by designating specific times for focused work. Setting boundaries during the day when digital interruptions are strictly forbidden can boost creativity and performance. Imagine this as a sacred time block, perhaps a couple of hours in the morning or post-lunch, dedicated entirely to any task requiring deep focus. Researchers have found that similar methods benefit dementia patients by adjusting built-in tech settings to conform to individual sensory needs (Dixon & Lazar, 2020). It's about finding that sweet spot where work can flourish without distraction. The goal is to craft a seamless transition from one environment or mental state to another, much like opening curtains to invite natural light into a room—the difference in ambiance is palpable and inspires a corresponding shift in productivity.

Creating a Distraction-Free Workspace

Creating a physical space specifically for focus is equally transformative. We're looking at places devoid of screens, buzzing alerts, or any electronic hums. This can be as simple as a desk in a quiet room, outfitted solely with essentials like paper, pens, and perhaps a window with a view. Taking cues from those with dementia who combat overstimulation using tailored auditory inputs, you, too, can craft a space that maximizes productivity through minimalism (Dixon & Lazar, 2020). The environment should whisper tranquility, inviting concentration and permitting your mind to wander only within the realms of creativity, not across digital landscapes.

Establishing Tech-Free Zones

Think of tech-free zones in your home or workplace where you can retreat to engage in deep work. In these zones, separation from digital devices is key. This separation provides cognitive rest, enhancing one's ability to engage with tasks at hand more deeply. Removing gadgets doesn't just free up physical space—it liberates mental clutter.

Engaging in Non-Digital Leisure Activities

Engaging in non-digital leisure activities serves as a refreshing counterpart to the overstimulation we often face. Reading physical books, partaking in hobbies like gardening, or embarking on leisurely walks connects us to the world beyond our screens. Each of these activities encourages mindfulness. Just as ID1 and ID11 utilize music through noise-canceling headphones in overstimulating environments, nature and literature here orchestrate a symphony of their own calm, refocusing the mind. These pursuits allow us to step back, glimpse the bigger picture, and rejuvenate our creativity.

Shifting Attention to Creative Hobbies

Leisure activities that don't require screens allow the brain to enter a state of rest and creativity, often blocked by digital overconsumption. Choosing to immerse oneself in a hobby shifts the brain's attention to different areas, fostering relaxation and innovative thinking becomes a canvas for unwinding, untethered notifications or virtual demands, allowing thoughts to marinate and ideas to ferment naturally.

Integrating Mindful Breaks

Consider integrating mindful breaks: time spent away from screens fosters moments of genuine human connection, ignites deeper thought processes, or simply invites peace. This can be as effortless as a ten-minute break outdoors and a chat over coffee. The idea is not far from how participants with dementia described the need to manage sensory input to prevent feeling overwhelmed (Dixon & Lazar, 2020). Our brains, too, require these mindful pauses to retain clarity and function optimally amidst a barrage of digital stimuli.

Creating Rituals in Dopamine-Free Zones

Engage actively with your environment by adding rituals to these dopamine-free areas. Perhaps the act of brewing tea or the scent of a candle can become intrinsic parts of engaging in deep work or leisure. This ritualization signals a shift in focus, akin to stretching before exercise—an invitation for the mind and body to prepare for a different tempo.

Nurturing Creative and Productive Habits

Being deliberate with these strategies can help build a mix of creative and productive habits. Acknowledging the struggle against digital overload and consciously choosing to divert some of this energy toward nurturing environments can create profound changes. While these changes require effort and commitment, they serve as potent antidotes against the ever-encroaching digital mire.

Remember, the digital world, much like any addiction, thrives on our craving for constant stimulation. Taking these conscious steps supports the creation of an internal and external landscape that champions productivity and well-being over overstimulation. So, let's welcome these tactics with enthusiasm, creating a new story where technology supports us instead of overwhelming our daily lives.

Concluding Thoughts

Have you ever mindlessly reached for your phone, only to realize that minutes have turned into hours? You're not alone. In our hyper-connected world, resisting the pull of digital devices can feel nearly impossible, but reclaiming control over your attention is achievable. This chapter discusses practical strategies to reduce digital distractions gradually, helping you foster a healthier relationship with technology and improve your focus and productivity.

To embrace a sustainable approach, consider implementing small changes rather than attempting a complete digital detox. For example, set specific times for social media use, creating a structured routine that minimizes impulse checking. Disable unnecessary notifications to regain command over your focus and manage the flow of information in your life. Additionally, filter your news consumption by following trusted outlets and limiting your engagement to specific times. These strategies can significantly enhance your mental clarity and reduce information overload.

Building on these small changes can lead to improvements in productivity and satisfaction, setting the stage for exploring innovative tools like the "Gray Screen" method to further combat digital addiction. As you integrate these strategies into your daily life, you'll discover a renewed appreciation for offline activities and a clearer path to achieving your goals.

But what if these initial adjustments merely scratch the surface? What if the key to transforming your productivity lies in an even deeper understanding of how your brain operates? Let's see how to fundamentally change the way you work, enabling you to achieve profound levels of concentration and creativity.

Chapter 6: Rewiring Your Brain for Deep Work and Focus

Imagine sitting down to work, but instead of focusing, you're overwhelmed by a flood of notifications and distractions. Every time you try to concentrate, your phone buzzes with alerts, or new emails pop up demanding your attention. You think you'll just check quickly, but before you know it, an hour has passed, leaving you feeling frustrated and unproductive. Many people wonder how some manage to stay focused while others struggle with constant interruptions, and you're not alone in this challenge.

This chapter dives into the art of rewiring your brain for deep work and focus. You'll discover a structured approach that can help enhance concentration and productivity, allowing you to achieve more in less time. Whether you're juggling a career, studies, or personal projects, the strategies outlined here aim to transform your work habits and train your mind for sustained focus amidst today's digital chaos.

The Deep Work Sprint

For high achievers, mastering focus amidst a sea of distractions becomes essential. Navigating through emails, social media, and unexpected interruptions can derail productivity. The Deep Work Sprint, a powerful method involving structured work sessions, targets this challenge. Using 90-minute focused work sessions, along with short breaks afterward, can really boost your concentration and productivity. This method helps you get more done in a shorter amount of time, making it perfect for entrepreneurs, professionals, students, and anyone looking to improve themselves.

During the Deep Work Sprint, follow these actionable steps to optimize productivity:

- **Set clear intentions:** Begin each session with a specific goal. For example, drafting three sections of a report or coding a feature. A well-defined objective provides direction and purpose.
- **Minimize distractions:** Silence notifications and alerts on digital devices. Consider utilizing apps like Freedom or Cold Turkey, which block distracting sites.
- **Create focused work blocks:** Allocate 90 minutes of intense, uninterrupted work. This mirrors a typical Pomodoro session but extends its duration to maximize depth in work.

- **Adopt a timer ritual:** Start with a timer to track each session. The ticking clock can serve as a gentle nudge back to task when focus wavers (Scroggs, 2021).
- **Conclusion through reflection:** Spend a few minutes reflecting on the session's output. Evaluate what went well and what diverted attention, and then calibrate goals for the next sprint.

Taking optimal breaks is crucial for maintaining productivity. During breaks, divert attention from work completely. Physical movement enhances mental recovery, so a brief walk or stretch contributes to a mental reset. Avoid turning to digital distractions during these breaks, as they can impair the return to focus (Team, 2023).

Next, creating your workspace enhances the effectiveness of each sprint. An ideal work environment is clean, uncluttered, and free from non-essential gadgets. Specific actions include:

- **Declutter regularly:** Write with minimal objects on the desk. Remove unnecessary items, keeping only essentials. This physical orderliness reflects in mental clarity.
- **Digital organization:** Organize folders and emails. Ensure digital tools and files are

systematically arranged, as digital clutter can be just as distracting.

- **Control acoustics:** Use noise-canceling headphones or play ambient sounds to drown out disruptive noises. Tools like Noisli or SimplyNoise offer adjustable soundscapes that aid concentration.

Additionally, when measuring progress, concentrate on assessing how efficient and high-quality each work session is. Track progress by:

- **Task logs:** Document tasks completed in each 90-minute block. Recording achievements reinforces discipline and illustrates cumulative progress.
- **Reflective assessment:** Devote several minutes post-session to analyze task quality. Consider what strategies worked and potential adjustments for future sprints, highlighting accomplishments alongside areas for improvement.

Developing structured work habits demands consideration of the balance between immediate gratification and long-term focus. This philosophical foundation can be introduced slowly without overpowering the practical steps, preparing the way for a more in-depth exploration in the next sections.

With each sprint, refine methods and approaches, finding what uniquely fits personal workflows and environments. Remember, clarity comes from structure, and depth emerges through disciplined focus. This cycle of work and reflection not only heightens productivity but also contributes to long-term professional and personal growth.

Training Your Brain to Crave Long-Term Rewards

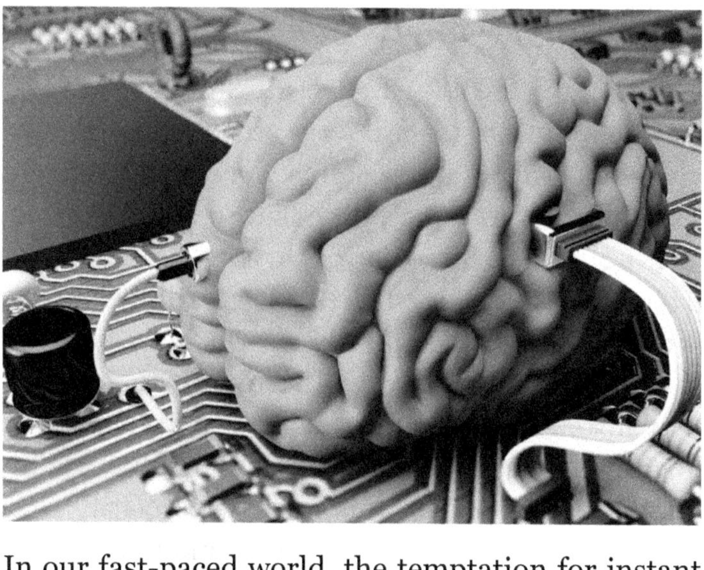

In our fast-paced world, the temptation for instant gratification can be hard to resist. Something like an exciting notification on your phone or the rush you get from a last-minute purchase gives you an immediate reward, triggering a flood of dopamine in your brain. Instant gratification is hard to resist because our brain's reward system is wired to favor immediate pleasure. The prefrontal cortex struggles to inhibit these urges, often losing out to the brain's amygdala, which oversees emotional responses and instant gratification. Adding to this is the ease of technology. It promotes a cycle of immediate rewards with its endless notifications and promises of quick satisfaction, keeping us caught in a web of distractions (Miller, 2019).

Cultivating a Mindset for Delayed Rewards

To counteract this urge, cultivating a mindset oriented toward delayed rewards is crucial. One effective way is to redefine success by moving beyond the urge for immediate results. Start by setting long-term goals that resonate deeply with you. Instead of focusing on the gratification of a finished product, savor the learning and growth processes that come with striving for those goals. For instance, rather than celebrating a temporary diet success, you could aim for a sustainable, healthy lifestyle. Recognizing this shift helps clarify what success means personally, transforming temporary setbacks into stepping stones toward significant achievement.

Breaking Down Long-Term Goals

To cultivate this mindset, break long-term ambitions into smaller, achievable tasks. Doing so creates a sense of accomplishment, sustaining motivation on the journey to greater goals. These milestones help by providing frequent reinforcement, keeping the brain's reward system engaged with positive yet delayed gratification. Prioritize long-term rewards that might not provide immediate dopamine hits, but over time strengthen neural pathways associated with patience and perseverance.

Daily Practice in Patience

See, daily practice in patience can significantly enhance productivity and focus over time. Start with simple exercises, like deferring checking your phone for thirty minutes during focused work sessions. By doing so, you're training your prefrontal cortex to regain control over the amygdala, reinforcing your ability to delay gratification. Another method is mindful meditation, which encourages staying present, increases awareness of impulses, and teaches the brain to resist them. Over time, these practices bolster resilience, promoting a pattern of long-lasting focus over fleeting disruptions.

Building Emotional Resilience

Maintaining patience isn't just about ignoring distractions; it requires emotional resilience to tolerate discomfort while pursuing ambitious goals. While it may feel strenuous at first, building this tolerance is essential for learning to resist instant rewards. Reflect on past challenges you've overcome. Recall moments when persistent effort, even in uncomfortable situations, guided you to success. You might recall a time in college, for example, when burning the midnight oil seemed unbearable, but persisting through it led to a rewarding career breakthrough. Such reflections heighten awareness of your capability to endure for substantial rewards instead of succumbing to ephemeral desires (*Master How to Delay Gratification and Level* Up *Your Life*, 2025).

This intrinsic reflection is key to rewiring our habits toward accepting delayed rewards. Below are exercises that can be instrumental in building this mental shift:

The Visualization Technique

Picture your long-term goal with clarity, engaging as many senses as possible. Imagine what it feels like to achieve that goal, the surrounding environment, even the tangible and emotional sensations accompanying its success. As a concrete example, visualize a personal goal like completing a marathon. Picture crossing the finish line, your muscles tired but your spirit triumphant, friends and family cheering, the air crisp against your skin. Steps for implementation include taking 5-10 minutes every day to visualize this goal in detail. Through consistent practice, this positive imagery becomes associated with perseverance, embedding a mental framework focused on delayed gratification.

Gratitude Journaling

Writing exercises help recognize past successes achieved by avoiding immediate gratification. Allocate time daily to note things you are grateful for that required sustained effort. An example would entail detailing how resisting impulsive buying enabled financial stability. Steps for implementation: each evening, jot down three accomplishments or moments of gratitude from the day linked to patience and persistence. Over time, reviewing these entries reinforces a positive blend of patience and sustained effort, reinforcing delayed gratification.

The 90-Day Challenge

Choose one long-term goal to focus on for 90 days, avoiding distractions related to competing with immediate gratifications. Concrete goals could range from learning a new language to consistently exercising. Steps for implementation involve setting a clear 90-day commitment plan, outlining specific daily actions, and maintaining a journal to record progress and setbacks. Review the journal bi-weekly to stay accountable and adjust strategies if necessary. Feel the progress accelerate over time, noticing how sustained focus enhances deep work and establishes a path to significant achievements.

Working through these exercises with dedication primes you for Monk Mode by gradually weaning off everyday distractions and laying a strong foundation for deep focus. This journey away from instant gratification and toward delayed rewards is a transitional process. It invites richer, longer-lasting fulfillment, emphasizing growth and resilience while setting the stage for advanced self-discipline strategies.

The journey might be rocky, but with these techniques and a shift in mindset, success isn't just a distant aspiration but a gradual, rewarding reality. By nurturing patience and perseverance, you build a framework for profound focus, helping you thrive amidst life's cacophony and bringing you ever closer to mastering the elusive art of deep work.

The Monk Mode Challenge

Monk Mode—sounds intriguing, right? If you're someone seeking to reach higher levels in your personal or professional life, it's a disciplined approach that might just be what you need. Essentially, Monk Mode involves adopting the habits of high achievers, focusing intensely on deep work while minimizing distractions. This strategy prioritizes delayed gratification over immediate rewards, helping you endure and succeed in tasks that require heavy concentration.

The Power of Deep Work

You've likely heard about deep work and its impact on productivity. Monk Mode takes this idea a step further by stressing the discipline required to maintain that focus over time. It's not just about being super productive; it's about completely changing how you tackle tasks so you can concentrate on valuable work without getting distracted by constant notifications or interruptions.

Habits of High Achievers

So, what do the habits of top performers look like? It's all about their daily routines and the commitment to stick to them. These high achievers create structured environments that minimize distractions. For example, think about elite athletes who wake up early to train. Their dedication pays off, showing how small daily commitments lead to big results. The improvements in concentration, productivity, and clarity from these routines are key to achieving great success.

Making the Commitment

To integrate Monk Mode into your life, start with a strong commitment—essentially, a promise to yourself. This means consciously deciding to set aside distractions and establishing clear boundaries between work and relaxation. Identify the specific distractions you want to eliminate, like mindlessly scrolling through social media or binge-watching shows during work hours. Define your work hours and clearly outline your relaxation times. This way, your brain knows when it's time to focus and when it's okay to unwind.

Building Accountability

Now, let's talk accountability. Sticking to a plan is easier when you have support. Consider reaching out to friends or joining groups focused on Monk Mode to create an accountability network. Having someone to check in on your progress can help keep you on track. Often, all it takes is that little accountability nudge to keep your motivation alive!

Creating a Distraction-Free Environment

Eliminating distractions is crucial. Use apps to block distracting websites during work hours and set up a workspace that's free from temptations. This space should be dedicated solely to deep work and inspire positivity, away from areas associated with relaxation. By doing this, you're training your mind to understand that entering this space means it's time to focus.

Balancing Intensity With Mindfulness

It might sound like a strict regime, but it's not just about shutting everything out. Part of Monk Mode's charm is balancing this intensity with mindfulness practices. Try incorporating meditation or deep breathing exercises before starting work. These techniques can calm your mind and reduce stress, making it easier to concentrate on complex tasks.

Starting Small

Ease into Monk Mode by starting small. Think of it like testing the water before diving in. Begin with shorter focus sessions and gradually increase the time as you get used to the routine. This method helps prevent burnout and keeps your motivation up.

Adapting Your Routine

When things get tough, be ready to adjust your routine to fit your needs. Remember, Monk Mode isn't about strict rules; it's about finding what works best for you. Maybe you'll discover that working in short bursts works better than long stretches, or perhaps breaking your day into focused blocks suits you more.

Setting Clear Goals

Clear, achievable goals act as a guide in your Monk Mode journey. Identify what you want to accomplish—whether it's progressing in your career, achieving academic goals, or fostering personal growth—while noting any obstacles. With clarity, prioritize your deep work sessions when you're naturally more productive, like early mornings or late at night.

Fostering Creativity

Reducing distractions creates an environment where creativity can thrive. When you minimize the noise and interruptions in your life, you make space for your mind to think clearly. This newfound clarity helps you focus better on your tasks and increases your overall productivity. With a clear mind, you're also able to tackle problems in new ways.

When distractions aren't pulling your attention in different directions, you're more open to fresh ideas and solutions. This can lead to innovative thinking, allowing you to see challenges from different angles that you might have missed before. Instead of feeling overwhelmed by everything on your plate, reducing distractions helps you engage fully with your work, inspiring you to think creatively and come up with unique solutions.

Balancing Solitude and Connection

While embracing Monk Mode, remember the potential for isolation. It's a notable caveat to keep in mind. Striking a balance between your need for alone time and social interaction is essential. Plan social downtime and schedule moments to connect with your support network to avoid falling into isolation.

Experiencing Transformation

As you get comfortable navigating Monk Mode, you might start noticing that meeting your goals becomes smoother and that your mind feels clearer. That's the transformation of rewiring your brain to value sustained focus over fleeting distractions. It's all about finding that sweet spot where discipline and relaxation coexist, keeping your productivity high and your stress levels in check.

In the next steps, consider exploring advanced techniques for sustaining long-term discipline in Monk Mode. It's an ongoing journey toward sharpening your focus and enhancing mental clarity, and adapting it to fit your life will only enrich your experience.

Final Thoughts

Imagine attempting to work, only to be overwhelmed by notifications and distractions. Every time you try to concentrate, your phone buzzes, drawing you away from your tasks. Many people struggle with focus in this distraction-filled environment, but you're not alone. This chapter explores how to rewire your brain for deep work and improved concentration, offering structured approaches to enhance productivity amid today's digital chaos.

The deep work sprint method is designed for those seeking to master focus. By implementing 90-minute work sessions followed by short breaks, you can significantly boost your productivity. Start each session with clear intentions, minimize distractions by silencing notifications, and create a dedicated workspace free from clutter. Tracking your progress through task logs will also help reinforce discipline and identify areas for improvement. Effective breaks—like stretching or taking a walk—can further enhance your mental stamina during these focused periods.

Moreover, training your brain to crave long-term rewards over instant gratification is essential in today's fast-paced world. Cultivating a mindset focused on delayed gratification means setting long-term goals and breaking down those ambitions into smaller, manageable tasks. Daily practices, such as deferring phone checks or engaging in mindful meditation, can strengthen your ability to delay gratification. By embracing a monk mode challenge, where you minimize distractions and prioritize deep work, you pave the way for significant personal and professional growth.

But what if the key to unlocking your motivation and maintaining long-term success lies in mastering the very essence of dopamine itself? What hidden strategies could empower you to take full control over your motivation, ensuring that your ambitions are not only achieved but also sustained? As we transition to the next chapter, prepare to harness your brain's reward system and transform your approach to goal-setting and achievement. Are you ready to unlock the secrets of dopamine and elevate your journey toward sustained motivation and success? The next phase of your growth is just around the corner!

Chapter 7: Mastering Dopamine for Motivation and Long-Term Success

In today's world, distractions are everywhere, making it feel like we're stuck on a hamster wheel of instant gratification. With just a swipe or a tap, our phones easily pull us into a vortex of notifications and endless scrolling, pulling us away from our important tasks. You sit down to work, but instead of focusing on what needs to be done, your attention drifts to anything but the task at hand. Those quick bursts of pleasure from completing a game level or receiving likes on a post can be so tempting. But the guilt quickly follows when you notice how much time has quietly slipped away without any real progress made.

For high achievers and professionals who strive for more, understanding what fuels our actions can be a game changer. In this chapter, we'll explore how mastering dopamine might just be the key to unlocking sustained motivation and long-term success, all while embracing challenges and finding balance.

The Dopamine Bank Account

Dopamine is an important part of our everyday lives, acting as a key player in motivation, reward, and how our brains work. Think of it as a messenger in your brain that guides you toward activities that promise happiness and fulfillment. For example, when tackling a work project or embarking on a fitness journey, dopamine fuels your motivation by making the anticipated rewards of completing these tasks feel truly rewarding. This neurotransmitter gets you moving, helping you go from being inactive to taking action. When we understand how dopamine works, we can see why some activities, like eating, feel so great and why addictive behaviors can be so tempting.

Dopamine and the Reward System

Dopamine does more than just motivate us; it's also a key part of the brain's reward system (National Library of Medicine, 2021). As you engage in enjoyable activities or even substance use, dopamine is released, creating positive reinforcement. For instance, the joy of a favorite meal or the sense of accomplishment after a successful workout can both cause a surge of this neurotransmitter. However, the problem comes when activities that should give you natural dopamine are replaced by habits that cause too much dopamine, like the overstimulation we get from modern technology. This overload can lead to dependency, making you crave these high-dopamine activities more and more.

The Need for Balance

Finding balance is essential. While dopamine helps us figure out what feels good, too much of it—especially from artificial sources—can cause problems. Engaging in activities like scrolling through social media or binge-watching shows can lead to a constant release of dopamine, creating an imbalance. Initially, these activities might seem harmless, but over time, they can leave you feeling restless and unable to concentrate. Your brain gets used to high dopamine levels, making everyday pleasures, like taking a walk or enjoying a book, feel less enjoyable. This sets off a cycle in which you need to engage in stimulating activities more frequently to feel the same amount of pleasure.

Managing Dopamine Levels

To manage dopamine levels, it's important to be mindful of what gives you pleasure. Techniques like dopamine fasting, although debated, reflect one approach to moderating dopamine production by taking breaks from activities that cause spikes in its levels. For instance, setting limits on screen time or scheduling regular periods of unplugged time can help recalibrate your brain's response to rewards. Furthermore, engaging in activities like meditation and yoga can heighten mindfulness, allowing you to enjoy the present moment without distractions and contribute to a more balanced dopamine response (Desai et al., 2024). These activities not only help manage dopamine but also improve overall mental well-being by reducing stress.

Setting Achievable Goals

In addition to lifestyle changes, understanding dopamine's interaction with motivation reveals deeper layers. The pursuit of goals, often driven by significant dopamine activity, highlights how incremental progress boosts motivation. For instance, setting small, achievable goals can lead to consistent dopamine releases, supporting sustained motivation towards long-term ambitions. This explains why breaking tasks down into manageable steps leads to success—each step gives you a little dopamine boost!

Practicing Mindful Consumption

Avoiding overstimulation requires discipline and thoughtful practice. One effective method is mindful consumption, where you consciously decide how to spend your free time. Choose activities that provide long-term satisfaction instead of just quick pleasures. Engaging with media intentionally fosters a more balanced lifestyle, supporting healthy dopamine flow. Activities like exercise or creative projects can stimulate dopamine naturally while keeping you aligned with your life goals.

The Habit Loop of Dopamine

Dopamine's role in reinforcing habits is another important aspect. When you take consistent actions that align with your meaningful goals, dopamine helps motivate you to keep going. Each step toward your desired outcome is rewarded with a dopamine release, reinforcing your habits and making it easier to continue.

As we shift our focus to understanding the psychological benefits of challenges, we uncover another side of dopamine. While it is invaluable in driving motivation and reward, the upcoming section delves into how overcoming challenges deepens our satisfaction. Facing difficulties enriches our experiences and personal growth in valuable ways. The journey through challenges offers its own rewards, teaching us that true contentment comes not just from instant gratification but also from the fulfillment of overcoming obstacles. Exploring these nuances helps us find healthier paths to long-term success and mental wellness, illustrating that meeting challenges head-on brings even greater rewards.

Desirable Difficulty

Understanding how the dopamine system works equips you with a valuable tool to tackle life's challenges. When you learn to manage your dopamine effectively, you build the strength to engage in tasks that may initially seem intimidating. We'll now explore the idea of "Desirable Difficulty," which shows how balanced dopamine levels can help you embrace and manage challenges effectively, especially after going through a dopamine detox. The end result? Cleansing your brain's reward system enables you to tackle challenges that once seemed overwhelming.

Embracing Desirable Difficulty

Desirable difficulty involves intentionally choosing challenges that are a bit harder than routine tasks. Why should you embrace difficulties? It may seem odd, but the rewards are significant. Struggling at first can lead to greater accomplishments, providing a joy that easy wins can't match. On the other side of these challenges lies personal growth and a deep sense of achievement.

Building Resilience Through Challenges

Tackling tough tasks builds resilience in both your mind and emotions. As you push through challenges, you develop a strong mindset that can deal with stress and adversity. This resilience isn't just for one-time situations—it creates a habit of perseverance that changes how you approach life. The sweetness of success becomes even more rewarding when you've worked hard for it. With balanced dopamine levels, your brain learns to appreciate the excitement of overcoming obstacles instead of becoming complacent.

Detoxing From Distractions

Part of this transformational process involves detoxing from distractions. When you cut back on the instant gratification that often pulls you away from meaningful work, you create room to pay attention to more demanding tasks. Quick distractions and easy rewards clutter your mind and make pursuing challenging goals harder. Detoxing resets your dopamine levels, restoring your brain's ability to seek out satisfaction beyond immediate pleasures. This change opens doors for more fulfilling achievements.

Finding Fulfillment

Imagine you've reduced your constant checks on social media. With fewer distractions, you can spend time engaging in rewarding activities, like reading challenging books or learning new skills. The confidence you gain from completing these tougher tasks boosts your motivation and sets you up for continued success. This detox helps shift your focus from quick rewards to lasting achievements.

Adopting a Growth Mindset

Your mindset is also critical in this process. Seeing challenges as chances for growth can change your entire outlook. Instead of viewing them as roadblocks, consider them stepping stones to your personal development. Every obstacle is an opportunity to learn and expand your skills. Encouraging yourself to adopt this perspective opens the door for challenges to become welcome experiences that help shape you into a more resilient and capable person.

Real-Life Examples of Growth

Everyday examples illustrate this principle beautifully. Take a student learning a new language; it might feel overwhelming at first—unfamiliar grammar, a new vocabulary, and tricky pronunciation. However, as they progressively master these challenges, the joy of holding a conversation in their new language far outweighs the allure of short-term distractions. The dopamine released during these achievements provides meaningful gratification that encourages continual growth.

In the workplace, this concept translates to taking on projects outside your usual expertise. While it can feel daunting, successfully tackling these projects can greatly enrich your skill set and boost your confidence. A software developer exploring machine learning not only expands their capabilities but also strengthens their self-belief. The dopamine released during this journey reinforces their ability to learn and adapt, even when treading into new territory.

Seeking Growth in Sports

Athletes are great examples of embracing challenges. They continually push their boundaries and endure the early struggles of mastering a new sport or refining their techniques. The eventual successes—like scoring a goal or achieving a personal best—bring immense satisfaction. This experience of overcoming challenges becomes addictive in a positive way as athletes learn to love testing their limits, knowing that each drop of sweat brings them closer to victory.

The Teacher's Challenge

Teachers also face the ongoing challenge of engaging students, constantly adapting their methods to spark interest and understanding. The effort they put into improving their teaching strategies ultimately pays off when students grasp complex concepts and express gratitude. This effort not only enriches the students' learning experiences but also gives teachers a deep sense of professional fulfillment.

As you work toward long-term success with the help of detoxed dopamine, keep in mind that mastering challenging tasks builds a solid base for boosting your ambition. By building resilience and enhancing your ability to manage challenges, you'll be prepared for what's ahead. In the next section, we will discuss how to use dopamine effectively to ignite even greater motivation and ambition, ensuring you stay focused and on track to achieve your goals.

How to Harness Dopamine for Drive, Ambition, and Mental Toughness

Dopamine's role in boosting motivation lies in its connection to excitement and reward. When we encounter something rewarding, dopamine surges in our brain, making us feel good and eager to seek that feeling again. Understanding this can fundamentally change how high-achievers, entrepreneurs, professionals, students, and self-improvement enthusiasts approach their goals. Our brains thrive on new experiences and successes, with dopamine acting as a signal of achievement.

Breaking Down Goals for Success

Setting rewarding milestones goes hand in hand with how dopamine functions. When you break your big goals into smaller, doable tasks, you're not just making them easier to tackle—you're also creating chances for dopamine to encourage you. This creates an internal reward system. Each time you reach a milestone, your brain releases dopamine, which motivates you to keep going. Goals that align with what matters most to you amplify your motivation, since dopamine's release is linked to feeling satisfied and making progress toward something meaningful.

Setting Meaningful Challenges

To maintain a steady release of dopamine, it's important to set milestones that matter to you and challenge you without making you feel overwhelmed. For example, this might mean scheduling regular reviews of your skills at work or aiming to get to a certain level in a new hobby. Each small success releases dopamine, pushing you to move forward.

Building Mental Toughness

Developing mental toughness is essential for staying motivated. Stepping out of your comfort zone helps, and facing challenges requires resilience. Embracing difficulties with a mindset focused on learning is key. Journaling can be a powerful tool here. Reflecting on your experiences helps you gain insights, recognize patterns, and spot areas for improvement. This practice can create a cycle of progress, as dopamine reinforces the lessons learned from setbacks.

Questions for Reflection

Ask yourself questions while journaling to guide your thoughts: What did I learn from today's challenges? How did I feel after reaching a goal? Where did I face setbacks, and what strategies can I try next time? Reflecting in this way promotes positive thinking and strengthens motivation.

Using Visualization to Enhance Focus

Incorporating visualization into your routine can boost dopamine's effects. Visualization involves mentally picturing your success, which mimics the dopamine surge you feel when achieving goals. Engage all your senses during this process; don't just visualize completing the task, but also feel the emotions that come with it. This technique increases motivation and helps you stay focused on your goals.

Celebrating Achievements

Motivation can fade if you don't take time to celebrate your achievements. Recognizing your progress connects dopamine release to your inner drive. Celebrating even small wins creates a sense of accomplishment and reinforces the behaviors you want to continue. Celebrations can be personal rewards, like taking a break, treating yourself, or sharing your achievements with supportive friends or family. Acknowledging your progress tells your brain that your efforts are valuable, making your motivation even stronger.

Practical Exercises for Motivation

Let's look at practical exercises to optimize motivation. Use dopamine's rewarding nature to strategize around setting clear, rewarding milestones that support your personal growth. For example, map out smaller, enjoyable tasks that lead toward a larger goal. This way, you can get consistent dopamine boosts from the rewards you earn along the way.

Setting Achievable Milestones

- **Identify primary goals:** Reflect on long-term aspirations and determine overarching missions.
- **Break goals into smaller tasks:** Dissect large goals into actionable steps, increasing ease and manageability.
- **Set short-term targets:** Align daily or weekly targets that are challenging yet rewarding.

Journaling for Reflection and Growth

- **Allocate regular time for reflection:** Choose a time that suits your routine, ensuring consistency.
- **Write about experiences:** Explore feelings, learnings, and areas of challenge.
- **Assess progress:** Regularly revisit journals to discern patterns and growth paths.

Visualization Techniques for Continuous Motivation

- **Envision success:** Take moments to visualize achieving goals vividly.

- **Engage senses:** Imagine not only sights but sounds, feelings, and surrounding environments.
- **Reflect on emotions:** Notice emotions that arise, associating them with eventual achievement.

Dopamine-driven practices motivate a proactive stance toward challenges by emphasizing both processes and achievements. Each small win builds momentum, enhancing resilience and motivation while reinforcing the cycle of improvement. As you incorporate these strategies into your life, you'll develop habits that leverage dopamine for lasting success.

Specially designed exercises offer fresh perspectives and deepen your understanding of how to use dopamine effectively. Each step clarifies what success looks like, boosts your mindset, and empowers your journey, all while focusing on steady and thoughtful progress. By grasping and applying the motivational cycle of dopamine, you actively create a path for growth and mastery, encouraging perseverance and fulfillment in everything you pursue.

Concluding Thoughts

In today's world, distractions lurk around every corner, pulling us into a whirlwind of instant gratification. Our phones, with their endless notifications and scrolling possibilities, pull our focus away from essential tasks, leaving us frustrated and unproductive. For those seeking to achieve more, grasping the concept of dopamine and its role in motivation can be transformative. This chapter explores how understanding and managing dopamine can help unlock sustained motivation, allowing individuals to embrace challenges and find balance in their lives.

Dopamine serves as a key player in our motivation and reward systems. It guides us toward activities that promise happiness and fulfillment, such as completing a project or engaging in a fitness journey. However, the problem arises when our reliance on digital technology leads to overstimulation and dependency on artificial sources of dopamine. To counterbalance this, it's essential to find equilibrium in our dopamine levels. Techniques such as setting time limits on screen usage, engaging in mindfulness practices, and breaking down long-term goals into smaller, achievable tasks can help manage dopamine effectively and enhance overall well-being.

But what happens when the distractions return, threatening to unravel all the progress you've made?

How can you build a solid barrier against the constant temptations that digital life imposes? The next chapter will reveal the strategies and mindset shifts necessary to create lasting systems of focus that protect your hard-won concentration.

Chapter 8: The Long-Term Strategy— Building a Fortress Against Distractions

Samantha, a passionate entrepreneur with her eyes set on launching a groundbreaking startup, found herself in a constant battle with distractions. Each day began with the best of intentions, filled with ambitious goals and a meticulously crafted to-do list. Yet, by midday, she often derailed—her focus shattered by endless notifications, unexpected calls, and frequent office interruptions. Despite these obstacles, Samantha would persist, hoping that tomorrow would be different. It was frustrating; she could feel the potential bubbling within her, but couldn't quite harness it consistently.

This struggle is all too familiar for many who balance demanding careers with personal growth quests. We understand the eagerness to achieve great things and the disheartening feeling when daily distractions thwart progress. Amidst this chaos, there lies hope. This chapter ventures deep into building an unyielding fortress against the tide of distractions, enabling Samantha—and readers like you—to stay disciplined and focused, paving the way for sustained success and mental clarity over the long term.

The Focus Fortress

Understanding the need for a strong strategy to stay focused and clear-headed in a world full of distractions requires following proven methods.

The Importance of Deliberate Attention

A solid focus strategy centers around the idea of intentional attention. This means setting up an environment and routine that encourages careful involvement with tasks. One key method to strengthen mental endurance and discipline is time blocking. This is when you set aside specific periods for focused work, which helps direct attention and reduce interruptions. Time blocks, whether for deep work or project management, create a structured way to dive into tasks. For instance, if you dedicate 9:00 to 11:00 AM daily for deep work, those hours can be spent at your best mental capacity (Buttimer Consulting, 2025).

Tracking Progress for Sustained Focus

Tracking progress is crucial for keeping sustained focus. By regularly checking productivity, people can see where changes might be needed. Observing focus patterns can show when you are most alert, helping to schedule demanding tasks during those times. Journals and productivity apps are great tools for recording daily successes and thoughts. They help you spot patterns of peak efficiency and tweak your strategies accordingly. This ongoing practice builds not only discipline but also clarity, keeping you on track for long-term goals and allowing for necessary adjustments (Eckert, 2023).

The Role of Breaks in Concentration

While intense focus is essential, taking breaks is also important for maintaining this high concentration over time without burning out. The brain requires rest and recovery periods to stay sharp. Breaks act as refreshers, clearing mental clutter and energizing the mind. These can be short, 5-minute breaks every 25 minutes, as suggested by the Pomodoro Technique, or longer breaks following extended focus periods. Engaging in light activities like a short walk or stretching during breaks can boost both mind and body, ensuring that productivity remains steady over time.

Managing Distractions Effectively

Distractions can come from within, like tiredness, or from outside sources, like phone alerts or interruptions from coworkers. To reduce distractions, it's important to set boundaries. Start by identifying these distractions and tackling them head-on. For example, placing a “do not disturb” sign on your desk or sharing your focus schedule with colleagues shows respect for your work time.

These measures create an environment that promotes concentration, where distractions are expected and managed, allowing for smooth transitions into deep focus.

Creating an Optimal Work Environment

Choosing a quiet, personalized workspace reduces sounds and visuals that can disrupt focus. Noise-canceling headphones or white noise can help block out background noise, further aiding concentration. Reducing visible distractions, like phone screens or unrelated tabs, can also lower the chances of being distracted. Organizing your workspace, from lighting to desk setup, can significantly influence your ability to maintain discipline and focus (Buttimer Consulting, 2025).

Coordinating Team Focus Time

Coordinating focus time among team members adds another layer to staying productive. Team focus time means that periods of deep work benefit not only individuals but also increase group productivity. This teamwork boosts overall output, similar to a sports team working together toward a common goal. Establishing team focus hours and having regular check-ins on progress and challenges make sure the full potential of focus time is realized. Rotating contact points during these blocks allows all team members to reach their highest concentration levels while keeping communication with stakeholders ensures that these focus periods are well-planned and respected.

As we move forward in this chapter, it's important to recognize the role of mindfulness practices, physical activity, and nutrition. These aspects create a well-rounded approach to maintaining mental sharpness and preparing the body for focused work. Embracing these practices builds resilience, ensuring that your focus fortress remains strong against the daily distractions you face. With thoughtful planning and careful strategies, you can gain the clarity necessary to effectively chase long-term goals.

The Dopamine-Proof Morning Routine

Building focus and maintaining it over time is a bit like crafting a sturdy fortress. No single element can stand alone. Just like in content management, you need a coherent system that fits seamlessly into your day-to-day life. Begin by recognizing the necessity of focus, as it forms the foundation for protecting yourself against distractions. Implementing time blocks can help recharge your mental energy, creating a productive rhythm that keeps distractions away.

To stay on top of priorities, plan your day by outlining tasks clearly. Identify what needs the most attention and align your daily goals with your long-term objectives. Each task becomes meaningful, contributing to bigger milestones, and enhancing productivity by ensuring your efforts have direction.

The Power of Morning Routines

The elements of morning routines—like meditation or mindful breathing—work like fortification layers that promote a calm and steady start. Engaging in physical activities primes your body for productivity, tying back to benefits like improved focus and emotional well-being. Consider these practices as your mind's warm-up routine before diving into the day's tasks.

Setting up effective morning routines involves consistent practice. Start by waking up with the same rhythm daily, even on weekends. Incorporate exercises like stretches or light yoga—these improve mood and elevate energy, helping you transition smoothly into a working mindset. Set aside just 10 minutes to connect with your body, noting physical sensations and any built-up tension to release.

Nutrition and Mental Clarity

Nutrition plays a central role in maintaining mental clarity. Start with a breakfast that supports cognitive function—think mixed grains or a protein-rich smoothie. These choices help avoid crashes that make your brain sluggish, keeping you alert instead.

Pair these routines with nutrition. Prepare a balanced breakfast ahead of time. A nutrient-rich meal, laying in fiber, fats, and proteins, fuels your morning's productivity. Staying hydrated also enhances cognitive sharpness, so drink a glass of water after waking. These small actions convey respect for your body's needs, supporting physical and mental well-being.

Mindfulness Exercises for Clarity

Let's look at examples of routine activities and their impact on mental clarity. A mindfulness exercise transforms your morning: sit comfortably, draw slow breaths, hold each for five seconds, and let your thoughts happen without judgment for a five-minute period. This practice offers mental clarity and reduced anxiety right at the start. You might adjust the breath focus period to better suit your schedule, a tweak that keeps the practice feasible and engaging.

Journaling for Progress Tracking

Explore journaling as a way to track your progress. It helps you with your self-improvement goals by letting you reflect on your achievements and challenges. Start each entry by writing down your plans for the day, including how you will tackle tasks and where you will focus your energy. This practice helps you stay aligned with your goals, especially when distractions come up.

These journaling habits help you develop a strong foundation for productivity and prepare your mind for complex tasks. With each step, your ability to focus grows stronger. There is power in discipline, and this is reflected in the consistent actions you take.

As you move forward, make sure to integrate the strategies we've discussed. Strengthening your morning routine through a mix of exercises builds discipline and enhances focus. Each practice builds on the last, creating a plan aimed at steady progress rather than rushing through distractions.

Each day will become a consistent yet flexible experience rooted in personal growth. It's not only about setting strict goals but also about creating an environment—internally and externally—that nurtures growth and creativity. When distractions arise, your structured discipline will remain strong, providing clarity and focus, supported by the habits you build over time.

Creating a Low-Stimulation Environment

Every morning, you dive into your day with a structured routine that boosts your brain's natural dopamine levels. This morning start not only energizes your body but also sets a mental rhythm to carry you smoothly through the day. As you transition from personal time to a focused work environment, make sure your workstation supports the mental clarity you've created in the morning.

The Power of Decluttering

Let's discuss the importance of decluttering. Imagine entering a workspace where everything unnecessary is gone. A clean desk allows fresh ideas to flow because your mind isn't distracted by visual clutter. Regularly removing items you don't need sharpens your focus and boosts creativity, like beginning each day with a blank canvas ready for your next masterpiece.

Managing Sensory Inputs

Recognize the value of managing sensory inputs. Soft lighting can transform your workspace, providing a soothing atmosphere that allows you to concentrate. Noise can steal your attention, so using noise-canceling headphones or soft background music can create an auditory shield that enhances productivity. Gentle tunes or white noise foster focus, creating a bubble where your best work can occur.

Incorporating Nature

Adding elements of nature to your workspace can greatly enhance its atmosphere, no matter its size. Plants improve air quality, reduce stress, and sharpen focus. Caring for a plant daily promotes self-discipline and offers small moments of calm, symbolizing your commitment to mental clarity and growth.

Setting Boundaries

Setting boundaries is crucial when working with others. It's not about being unapproachable; it's about protecting the focus you've worked hard to achieve. Communicate your needs clearly, whether with a simple “do not disturb” sign or by letting colleagues know your deep work hours. Non-verbal signals, like wearing headphones, can indicate your need for focus without saying a word. These small actions establish dedicated times in a chaotic day.

Your Environment as an Ally

Your environment supports your focus and discipline. It should reflect your personal style while nurturing the clarity you create each morning. Every item in your workspace should serve a purpose or inspire you. Emphasizing minimalism reduces both physical and mental clutter, steering your focus back to what truly matters.

Creating a Low-Stimulation Environment

To cultivate a low-stimulation environment, focus on adjusting sensory inputs that promote productivity. Surrounding yourself with greenery is not just about aesthetics; it nurtures your senses and enhances your well-being. The subtle diversity of nature can foster clarity and relaxation, helping creativity flourish.

Experimenting With Lighting

Experiment with lighting to create the ideal workstation. Natural light boosts productivity, but when it's not available, use warm-toned lamps to mimic it. A well-lit space keeps your energy up and thoughts clear, while dim environments can lead to fatigue and distraction.

Navigating Work-Personal Boundaries

The balance between work and personal time deserves attention. Many find it challenging to navigate this boundary, but tools like task timers and digital well-being apps can help you stay on track. Using a visible schedule to map out your tasks provides clarity and reinforces discipline.

Gaining Control Over Your Space

For those balancing remote work or various responsibilities, having control over your environment enhances your day. Spaces designed to minimize sensory overload support mental clarity and lead to a greater sense of accomplishment. With every improvement, you'll find that tasks flow more smoothly, stress becomes manageable, and creativity has room to grow.

The Ongoing Journey of Focus

Maintaining focus and mental clarity requires continuous adjustments and conscious effort. The aim isn't perfection but steady progress. When a new strategy works well, take note of it. Identify what clicks and what needs tweaking, allowing your environment to evolve in response to your needs.

The Impact of Workspace Design

Discussions about workspace design often overlook the significant effect on your environment has on mental well-being. When we create a space focused on simplicity, nature, and clear boundaries, we honor the work we produce and the individuals we aspire to become. Your workspace is an ally in your quest for enhanced focus and reduced distractions.

In crafting such environments, we create a place where discipline meets efficiency, and creativity leads to success. This is the fortress we establish against constant distractions—a space where focus thrives, and external noise fades into the background.

Summary and Reflections

This chapter delves into building an unyielding fortress against distractions, enabling you and individuals like Samantha to cultivate sustained focus and mental clarity necessary for long-term success. A strong strategy for maintaining focus involves establishing intentional attention through practices like time blocking. This method helps segment time into focused work periods, allowing for uninterrupted concentration. Aside from that, tracking progress and observing productivity patterns helps to better schedule demanding tasks during peak mental alertness. Regular breaks are equally crucial, requiring moments of rest and rejuvenation to optimize concentration.

Additionally, effectively managing distractions, creating an optimal workspace, and coordinating team focus time enhance overall productivity while building a supportive environment for deep work. Lastly, the journey toward building this focus fortress continues through the implementation of mindful practices, engaging in physical activity, and prioritizing nutrition. Developing a structured morning routine that includes mindful breathing or light exercise sets a positive tone for the day ahead.

Proper nutrition fuels cognitive function for productivity, while mindfulness exercises promote mental clarity. As distractions decrease and focus strengthens, implementing a low-stimulation environment also aids in maintaining clarity.

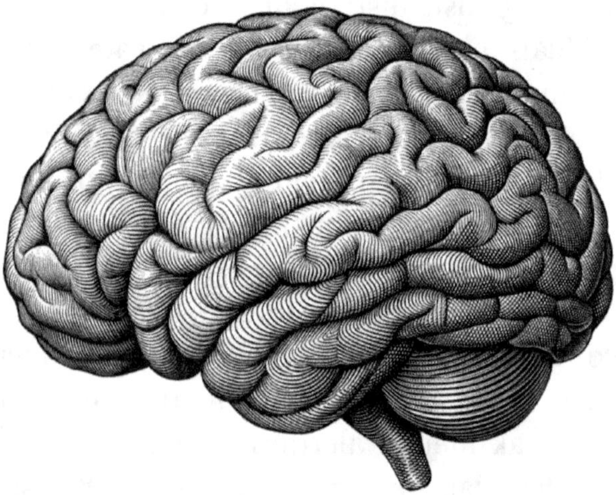

However, as you stand at the precipice of this fortress, a deeper challenge looms on the horizon: the incessant pull of the dopamine trap—an enticing yet perilous cycle that threatens to unravel all your hard-earned focus. What if the very tools that promise productivity also hold the key to a modern addiction, one that leads you to question whether true escape is even possible? Can you forge a path away from instant gratification to uncover the secrets of unyielding focus and regain control over your mind? The answer lies just beyond the next page, waiting to be discovered.

Chapter 9: Escaping the Modern Dopamine Trap Forever

Imagine a typical weekday morning. The alarm buzzes, and even before you're fully awake, your hand reaches out to silence it. Soon after, you're scrolling through social media, checking emails, or diving into the latest news feed—all happening before you've even set foot out of bed. This routine feels all too familiar for many of us, an unconscious habit propelled by the little dopamine hits from each notification and update. We often find ourselves caught up in this digital routine without really thinking about it, chasing after those brief moments of pleasure that keep us connected to our devices.

But what if this constant chase for the next digital high is quietly stealing away more than just our time? It can affect our mental clarity, productivity, and peace of mind. In this chapter, we'll explore practical strategies to break free from the compelling pull of technology, focusing on identifying and reshaping our relationship with dopamine. See, when we change how we interact with modern distractions, we'll uncover ways to reclaim our focus and transform our everyday lives.

Strategies for Controlling Technology and Building Resilience

Dopamine feedback loops significantly influence how modern technology captures our attention. These loops rely on our brain's reward system, where actions that release dopamine—like receiving likes on social media create pleasurable feelings. It's easy to see why a notification on our phone becomes so enticing; our brains associate these alerts with a dopamine rush, keeping us glued to our screens in search of the next moment of satisfaction. Understanding this mechanism sheds light on why unplugging can be such a challenge, even when we know it's necessary.

Identifying Personal Triggers

The first step is to recognize personal triggers that drive compulsive tech use. Reflect on whether boredom, stress, or specific environments lead you to reach for your phone. Children copying adults by checking their phones during family meals illustrates how curiosity connects to learned behaviors. Pay attention to when you often pick up your phone or unlock your device. Keeping a trigger journal can help reveal patterns; note the context each time you engage with your device. This journal can clarify the surroundings and emotions tied to technology use, helping to untangle your responses.

Establishing Tech-Free Zones

Creating tech-free zones in your home is another effective strategy. Start small by designating one room, such as the dining area or bedroom—as device-free. Even brief breaks from screens without the constant hum of notifications can noticeably shift your mood and perception. Gradually expand these zones over time. Reducing tech-reliant areas enhances deeper interactions and strengthens your resolve against the urge to check your devices. You might find that focus and clarity lead to better conversations and a calming atmosphere in these spaces, promoting fewer tech-dependent moments in other areas of your life.

Managing Screen Engagement

Now, let's discuss strategies to actively manage screen time. Take small steps by setting specific boundaries using available tools. Numerous apps can monitor screen time and establish usage limits. Consider apps that lock access to your device after a set amount of time. When you set boundaries for breaks from technology, you reclaim time for reflection and creativity, greatly enhancing your quality of life beyond mindless app switching.

Practicing Mindfulness in Digital Consumption

Mindfulness is vital when interacting with technology. Embrace conscious consumption by intentionally curating your digital diet. Before opening an app, pause and ask yourself: Is this activity enriching? Make a list of websites, channels, or platforms that enhance your curiosity or growth, and avoid mindless browsing. Replace scrolling with thoughtful engagement to find purpose in your digital interactions.

Building Resilience Against Distractions

To fortify your focus against the allure of technology, engage in activities centered around mindfulness. Simple daily meditation practices, even brief five-minute sessions, can be highly beneficial. Find a quiet spot, concentrate on your breathing, and gently redirect your thoughts back to your breath when they wander. Over time, these micro-practices will build your mental stamina.

Acknowledging Progress and Reflecting on Achievements

It's essential to reflect on and acknowledge your progress each time you reduce screen time or enhance your concentration. Each small victory paves the way for more significant, long-term changes. While this section highlights tactical methods, remember that these habits provide a foundation for a sustainably balanced digital experience.

In upcoming conversations, we'll take a closer look at how you connect with activities that trigger dopamine, helping you build lasting habits. These will assist you in finding a balance between technology and daily life, promoting mental clarity and strength. For now, changing how you interact with technology through practical steps is the first step in this journey of change.

Conducting a Monthly Dopamine Audit

Examining behaviors that trigger dopamine is key to breaking free from distractions. In our tech-heavy world, where every ping, like, and notification can cause a dopamine release, it's easy to get caught in a loop that leads us far from our goals. The secret to avoiding these traps lies in being aware of our habits and regularly assessing their impact on our lives. One helpful tool for this is the dopamine audit, which helps you assess your relationship with activities that spike dopamine and make the necessary adjustments.

Conducting a Dopamine Audit

The dopamine audit starts by listing daily habits that trigger dopamine. Make a simple list of everything you do in a day that might provide a dopamine boost, like scrolling through social media, watching videos, snacking without hunger, or excessive online shopping. Ask yourself what activities make you feel immediate pleasure but might not align with your long-term goals. It's about picking apart your everyday actions to see what's beneficial and what's just stealing your time and attention.

Reflecting on Your List

Once you have your list, reflect on how each activity aligns with your personal objectives. Be honest about whether these quick dopamine hits truly enhance your life or just offer temporary happiness. For example, spending numerous hours on social media might prevent you from completing that course you purchased to advance your career (Bromberg-Martin et al., 2010). Understanding this is crucial for changing behaviors that may not have been obvious until you list them.

Monthly Check-Ins

Every month, set aside time to conduct this audit. Create a set schedule for monthly assessments to ensure consistency. During this time, ask yourself key reflective questions: Are my current habits bringing me closer to my goals? Am I spending my time in ways that truly matter? What unnecessary habits can I cut down on? Use these questions to remain on track and make positive changes.

Setting Actionable Goals

After each audit, set specific and achievable goals. Identify a few changes you can make, such as reducing screen time or dedicating more time to activities that reflect your passions. It's not about making drastic changes overnight; instead, focus on small, meaningful adjustments that help you regain your focus and motivation. Creating a vision board can help reinforce your commitment. Use this board to visualize your desired lifestyle, highlighting priorities like healthier hobbies and positive content instead of mindless scrolling. Seeing your goals visually can be motivating and serve as a reminder of what matters to you (Lewis et al., 2021).

Enhancing Accountability

Accountability can make your audit even more effective. Connect with a support system, like a mentor, community group, or accountability buddy, to share your progress and goals. Regularly discussing your achievements and challenges creates a feedback loop that keeps you engaged in your personal growth. Working with someone who is also pursuing similar goals can be particularly helpful. For example, if they struggle with binge-watching shows or aimless social media scrolling, you can support each other and celebrate successes, making it easier to stay committed and avoid slipping back into old habits.

Through this process, you learn to consciously manage dopamine-driven activities instead of reacting to them. You gain the ability to make choices that align with your goals rather than falling into the trap of instant gratification offered by modern distractions. In the next section, you'll discover how maintaining your energy and focus can help transform these insights into lasting productivity. See, when you reassess your relationship with dopamine, your daily actions continue to align with a meaningful and rewarding life, driven by your goals rather than fleeting dopamine fixes.

Sustaining Energy, Focus, and Willpower

Throughout Life

Nutrition and lifestyle choices significantly influence our brain health and ability to focus. Eating a balanced diet packed with whole foods like leafy greens, nuts, and fish improves cognitive function. These foods provide crucial nutrients such as omega-3 fatty acids and antioxidants, which support your brain's optimal performance. To naturally incorporate these foods into your daily routine, consider starting your day with a protein-rich breakfast full of healthy fats, like an omelet with spinach and avocado. This will help fuel your brain for a productive day ahead.

The Role of Exercise in Mental Acuity

Exercise not only keeps your body fit but is also essential for enhancing mental sharpness and overcoming procrastination. Regular physical activity boosts blood flow to the brain, which improves focus and cognitive abilities. Simple changes to your daily routine, like taking quick brisk walks during breaks or adding yoga stretches, can break up monotony and refresh your mind. Imagine using a 10-minute walk to spark creative thinking or solve problems, turning what some may see as wasted time into a strategic break.

Utilizing the Pomodoro Technique

In terms of productivity methods, the Pomodoro Technique stands out for improving time management and prioritization. This technique involves selecting a task, setting a timer for 25 minutes of focused work, followed by a 5-minute break. After completing four of these cycles, you take a longer break of 15 to 30 minutes. As you break larger tasks into smaller, manageable sections, the Pomodoro Technique reduces feelings of overwhelm and increases focus. For example, a writer could use this method to draft parts of an article, keeping the work engaging while sustaining momentum. It helps prevent burnout and ensures steady progress across various fields.

Building Willpower and Mental Clarity

Developing willpower and enhancing mental clarity through daily practices like affirmations and mindfulness can lead to powerful changes in behavior. Start each day with positive self-talk that centers on your goals and reinforces a mindset dedicated to discipline and focus. This could be as simple as affirming that you will tackle challenges confidently or assuring yourself of your abilities before starting work. Pair these affirmations with short meditation sessions; just a few minutes a day of focused breathing or guided meditation can help clear your mind and boost concentration. These practices aren't about escaping reality but about facing it with a clearer mindset.

The Importance of Rest and Recovery

Rest and recovery are essential for maintaining consistent productivity. Taking breaks isn't just a luxury; it's a necessity. Scheduling downtime helps prevent burnout and ensures your brain has time to recharge. Consider adopting good sleep habits to enhance your energy and focus. Develop a bedtime routine that encourages relaxation, like reading a good book, avoiding screens before sleep, and ensuring your sleeping space is peaceful and tidy. Many people report significant improvements in energy levels and focus once they make sleep a priority. High achievers often find that better sleep leads to improved decision-making and sharper thinking.

Creating a Toolkit for Energy and Focus

Together, these strategies create a toolkit for maintaining high energy and focus. From nutrition to mental conditioning, these approaches are about building habits that empower you to take control of your concentration. Each strategy plays a vital role in providing a comprehensive path to improved mental sharpness and stronger willpower, helping you steer clear of modern distractions. By following these techniques, you'll gain the resilience to thrive in the face of daily stressors. In the next section, we'll bring these strategies together to guide you in permanently reclaiming your focus and mental clarity.

Bringing It All Together

To counteract the overwhelming pull of technology, it is crucial to understand how dopamine feedback loops influence our attention. Every notification triggers a release of dopamine, reinforcing our desire for immediate gratification and making it challenging to unplug. A productive first step is to identify personal triggers that compel you to reach for your devices. Keeping a trigger journal enables you to document the situations and feelings that lead to compulsive tech use. This process is beneficial to recognize and modify these patterns.

On top of that, implementing strategies such as creating tech-free zones in your home, managing screen engagement, and practicing mindfulness can enhance your ability to focus. For instance, designating specific areas—like the dining room or bedroom—as device-free can cultivate deeper relationships and improve your overall well-being. More structured approaches, like the Pomodoro Technique, can further enable you to maintain focus by breaking work periods into manageable segments, followed by scheduled breaks for recovery.

What's more, conducting a monthly dopamine audit allows you to assess your relationship with activities that cause dopamine spikes and make necessary adjustments. Reflecting on your daily habits and aligning them with your long-term goals can help maintain accountability and foster mindful consumption. Strategies such as proper nutrition, regular exercise, and an emphasis on rest and recovery all contribute to enhanced mental acuity and focus, providing a robust toolkit for combating distractions.

Yet, as you embark on this transformative journey, a profound question emerges: What is the true cost of reclaiming control over your mind and daily life? Can you truly abandon the comforts of immediate pleasure for a more fulfilling existence? The path toward becoming the new you, with a renewed mindset and approach to work and life, is fraught with challenges and revelations that await you just ahead. Will you take the leap?

Chapter 10: The New You: How Dopamine Detox Transforms Your Mindset, Work, and Life

David sat alone at his desk, the soft glow of his computer screen illuminating his tired eyes. He had a big presentation due in a few days and a mountain of work to plow through. Despite his best intentions, he found himself toggling aimlessly between social media tabs and checking his phone for notifications he didn't even care about. Each ping dragged him deeper into procrastination, and within moments, the anxiety hit. Why couldn't he just focus? David realized he was trapped in a cycle of distractions that seemed impossible to break—a common struggle for many high achievers today.

In our fast-paced world, we all seek ways to improve focus and productivity, but often fall victim to the relentless temptations of digital distractions. This chapter looks at these challenges and explores how a dopamine detox can change your mindset and lifestyle for the better. By learning about the benefits of regular detox practices, you can take back control of your attention and create a path toward achieving meaningful goals.

Reasons and Strategies for Sustaining Dopamine Detox

In the pursuit of excellence, high achievers often find themselves stuck in a cycle of distractions, procrastination, and overstimulation, which can hinder a dopamine detox. This detox is essential for resetting the brain's reward pathways and requires focus that comes from recognizing and addressing personal triggers. When bombarded with notifications, social media alerts, and digital temptations, it's crucial to identify what sparks these distractions.

The issue isn't just having distractions; it's also about the deeper triggers, like boredom or anxiety, that create a need for immediate dopamine hits.

Recognizing these internal and external triggers is the first step in creating a personalized plan that promotes mindfulness and intentional living.

Creating a Distraction-Free Environment

Successful detoxers prepare by creating an environment that reduces distractions, allowing them to focus on important tasks. Start by looking at your surroundings and opting for a minimalistic setup free of clutter that could divert your attention. This thoughtful removal of potential distractions involves planning, such as setting specific times to check emails or social media to prevent constant interruptions. For example, reorganizing your workspace with designated areas for different tasks can enhance focus. Ditch the idea of multitasking, which can reduce efficiency, and focus on one task at a time to improve work quality and satisfaction.

Preparation Is Key

Preparation serves as a cornerstone for navigating a dopamine detox. Without a structured plan, the best intentions can fall apart. To counter this, consider drafting a daily schedule that includes a balanced mix of work, rest, and leisure. Structuring your day not only promotes productivity but also ensures you receive adequate rest, maintaining consistent energy levels and mental clarity. While developing this schedule, make sure to include activities that support growth and well-being, encouraging a healthy relationship with dopamine-releasing activities without overdoing it (Gateway Foundation, 2019).

Building a Support System

Involving trusted friends, mentors, or communities as part of your support system offers accountability and encouragement. Sharing your detox journey with others not only provides a sense of solidarity but also exposes you to different perspectives and strategies. Friends or accountability partners can check in with you regularly, helping you stay committed to your plan while offering support during challenging moments. This collaborative approach mirrors the mutual aid described in effective abstinence interventions (Center for Substance Abuse Treatment, 2018).

Setting Realistic Expectations

It's also important to set realistic expectations, understanding that change takes time. Unrealistic expectations can lead to disappointment when progress isn't immediate. Instead, aim for small, achievable goals that contribute to your overall objectives. Celebrate these milestones, however small they may seem. This practice boosts morale and reinforces the positive aspects of gradual change. By focusing on long-term benefits instead of instant gratification, you can develop a healthier relationship with dopamine triggers (Gateway Foundation, 2019).

Exercise: Creating a Daily Schedule for Dopamine Detox

Step 1: Prioritize Key Activities

Define the primary tasks you seek to achieve each day. These should align with your long-term goals and require the most focus. For instance, if you're working on a major project, allocate peak productivity hours for deep work, avoiding unnecessary meetings or phone calls.

Step 2: Allocate Time for Breaks

Schedule short breaks between tasks to reset and recharge. Consider techniques such as the Pomodoro Technique, which involve working in short sprints, followed by brief rest intervals, to maintain high levels of concentration and stifle procrastination tendencies.

Step 3: Integrate Social and Personal Time

Ensure your schedule includes time for engaging with family, friends, and leisure activities. Balance fosters satisfaction and prevents burnout. Activities like taking a walk, meditating, or pursuing a hobby encourage relaxation without overwhelming dopamine stimulation.

Step 4: Reflect and Adjust

At the end of each day, review your accomplishments and challenges. Reflect on what worked well and where you encountered obstacles. Use these insights to adjust your schedule, making improvements that help tackle recurring issues effectively.

Developing new habits goes beyond just a dopamine detox; it involves embracing a growth mindset and a commitment to continuous self-improvement. As you incorporate these ideas into your life, you'll notice that the disciplined and structured approach you used during the detox can help speed up the formation of productive habits, influencing different areas of your personal and professional life.

Addressing the common challenges of this detox method with realistic planning and community support creates a foundation for significant change. This preparation aligns perfectly with your goals for a fulfilling, efficient, and satisfying life journey.

Internal Transformation for Focus and Discipline

Adopting a growth mindset is transformative for maintaining focus and discipline post-detox. When you begin to see challenges not as insurmountable problems but as opportunities for learning and growth, you open yourself up to continuous improvement. Say you're working on a project and hit a wall. Instead of viewing this as a failure, consider it an opportunity to refine your strategies or enhance your skills. This aligns with the concept of viewing setbacks as a chance to strengthen arguments, much like receiving critical feedback on a manuscript (Riaz Laghari, 2024).

The Importance of Self-Reflection

Self-reflection plays a crucial role in this process. Taking the time to review what led to certain outcomes can provide valuable insights. Keep a journal to jot down thoughts and experiences, which can help you identify patterns and make necessary adjustments for future success.

Creating New Habits for Sustained Focus

Creating new habits is essential for sustaining focus and can dramatically improve concentration. Consider the story of how regular writing sessions became the game-changer for completing a book, instead of squeezing in writing whenever there was a free moment, setting a routine led to productivity. For your daily work, establish a specific time for particular tasks, whether it's morning reading or afternoon brainstorming sessions. You're not simply creating a schedule, but intentionally designing one that matches natural energy levels throughout the day.

Using Habit-Tracking Tools

Habit-tracking tools can be incredibly helpful during this stage. Apps like Sanvello track your mood and offer mental wellness strategies. A habit tracker helps you stay accountable and shows what's effective and what isn't. Look for patterns in your productivity and adjust your schedule as needed.

Practical Exercises for Mindset Reinforcement

Now, let's explore practical exercises to reinforce this mindset shift. For instance, creating a vision board where you visually outline your goals and the steps needed to achieve them can significantly strengthen your focus. Gather images and words that resonate with your desired outcomes and place them in a prominent location. This visual roadmap keeps your goals top of mind daily, acting as a constant reminder of the bigger picture.

Practicing Daily Affirmations

Another useful technique is practicing daily affirmations. This involves repeating positive statements that support your goals and mindset. Start by identifying areas where you wish to improve or grow. Then create affirmations that challenge any existing beliefs or limitations. For example, a student might say, "I am capable of absorbing complex information and using it effectively in exams." Make it a habit to repeat these affirmations each morning, customizing them to match your lifestyle and current challenges for maximum relevance and impact.

Limiting Distractions

Limiting distractions is another key element of post-detox discipline. Setting boundaries around screen time is important for achieving this. Establish clear rules about when and where screens can be used, and engage in activities that allow your mind to disconnect from constant digital interaction. For instance, having a no-phone hour before bed can greatly improve your sleep quality, which is essential for maintaining focus (Riaz Laghari, 2024). Also, consider cultivating hobbies that require active engagement, such as playing an instrument or painting, which redirect focus and foster creativity while reducing stress.

Building a Support System

Creating a support system is vital. Connect with peers or mentors who understand your journey and can provide guidance and accountability, similar to how mastermind groups offer support and motivation. Regular check-ins with these individuals or groups can reignite motivation, particularly on difficult days.

Managing Burnout

To prevent burnout, it's important to adjust your workload expectations. Break tasks into smaller, manageable pieces to avoid feeling overwhelmed. Techniques like the Pomodoro Timer can help, ensuring you have balanced periods of focused work followed by short breaks. This method adds discipline to your workflow, promoting sustained attention while preventing exhaustion.

Practicing Gratitude

Finally, practice gratitude to cement these changes. Reflecting daily on what you've achieved and the positives in life nurtures a sense of fulfillment and purpose. You could maintain a gratitude journal or share these reflections with peers, not only fostering personal growth, but also enriching relationships in your support network.

When you implement these strategies and exercises into your daily life, you lay a strong foundation for focus and discipline. These initial changes become the basis for ongoing success. In the next section, we will explore more techniques and mindsets that will help you maintain momentum and resilience on your journey toward personal and professional achievement.

Techniques for Long-Term Dopamine Management

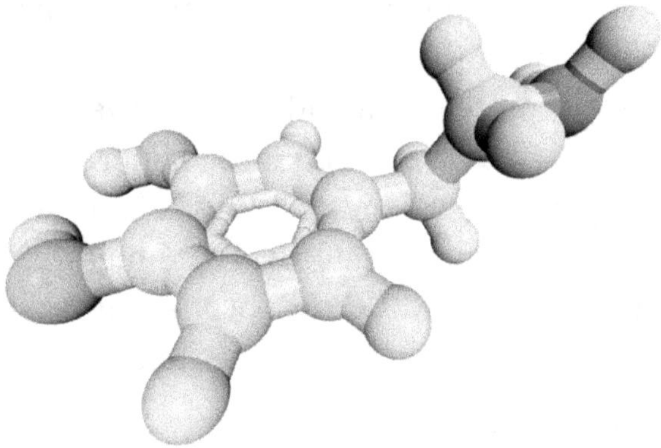

In a fast-paced world filled with distractions, a dopamine detox serves as a guide for achieving lasting focus. After the detox, it's crucial to refine your mindset, work habits, and lifestyle. This involves adopting techniques that sharpen your mind and nurturing habits aligned with your ultimate goals. This journey provides fulfillment for high-achievers, professionals, and students by fostering a growth mindset, successful habits, and the visualization of aspirations.

The Role of Mindfulness

Mindfulness serves as an anchor in this journey. Mindfulness meditation, for instance, is more than just a practice; it's a lifestyle choice for the conscious high-achiever. Integrating mindfulness meditation into daily routines acts much like a mental workout. You sharpen awareness by opting for brief sessions in the morning or before bed, making it part of your routine. Simply focusing on the breath deepens concentration and presence.

Breathing techniques, on the other hand, become your toolkit during overwhelming moments. You might encounter situations at work or school where stress peaks, and here's where you can apply a quick breathing exercise. Inhale deeply, hold for a moment, and exhale slowly. Repeat a few times until a sense of calm reappears. This practice redirects attention and aids in regaining focus naturally.

The Power of Continuous Learning

Continuous learning is your secret weapon to maintaining ambition. The world keeps spinning, technologies evolve, and staying relevant requires openness to new knowledge. Start with step-by-step methods, like attending workshops, subscribing to self-improvement literature, or joining skill-focused groups. Begin by assessing areas of improvement or interests. You might consider blocking time on your calendar for a monthly workshop.

These workshops introduce fresh perspectives, empowering you to connect trends with your projects. Delve into self-improvement books, devoting just 20 minutes daily. Joining groups that focus on specific skills like coding or communication expands your network and knowledge base. Such engagement fosters growth, reminding you of your purpose and ambition.

Regular Self-Assessment

Regular self-assessment becomes the compass for your journey. It's about understanding where you stand and where you aim to be. Setting aside dedicated time for self-reflection is crucial. Consider scheduling a weekly hour to journal personal development. Document your experiences, challenges, and advancements. This act of writing provides clarity and reinforces learning. Seeking feedback from valued peers adds an external perspective to your reflection. Constructive insights can reveal blind spots or provide an extra push where it's needed. You could create quarterly meetings with mentors or peers, gathering insights into how you're perceived in professional circles.

A Transformative Example: Sarah's Journey

Consider Sarah, a project manager at a bustling tech start-up. She initially grappled with managing her workload and maintaining a work-life balance. By integrating mindfulness meditation into her daily routine, she began each day centered and focused. Breathing exercises became her go-to method, easing moments of overwhelm during intense meetings or approaching deadlines.

As Sarah expanded her knowledge by attending workshops and diving into self-improvement literature, her confidence in managing teams grew. Self-assessment practices guided her, uncovering areas she excelled in and those needing attention. Seeking feedback from peers offered valuable insights and recognition of her growing expertise. Sarah's shift was palpable; she managed stress better, her productivity soared, and she fostered a supportive team environment that thrived under her leadership.

Final Insights

Identifying various triggers—whether they are external notifications or internal feelings like boredom—is essential for building a more mindful approach to life. Above all, creating a distraction-free environment is a key strategy in this process. This entails organizing your workspace and establishing designated times for technology engagement to minimize interruptions.

Preparation is vital, as drafting a structured daily schedule that balances focused work and restorative breaks can greatly improve mental clarity.

Additionally, building a support system of trusted friends or mentors can provide accountability and encouragement, enriching the detox experience with a sense of community.

Besides, setting realistic expectations and concentrating on small, achievable goals is vital for maintaining motivation. Daily reflection through journaling can offer insights into progress and areas needing adjustment. Techniques such as the Pomodoro Technique can enhance focus by breaking work into manageable intervals separated by breaks, while mindfulness practices promote resilience against distractions. Emphasizing a balanced lifestyle through proper nutrition and exercise further supports cognitive function. Once you adopt a growth mindset and consistently assess your journey, you can transform challenges into learning opportunities, ultimately paving the way for a fulfilling and focused life.

Conclusion

As we conclude this enlightening journey, it's important for us to pause and reflect on the promises we've made to ourselves and how we can implement the invaluable insights we've gained along the way.

Throughout our exploration, we have uncovered the pervasive and disruptive impact of modern distractions in our lives—those endless notifications that ping and ding, along with the captivating allure of social media platforms. These distractions often hinder our ability to concentrate on what truly matters, pulling our attention away from our goals and aspirations. However, the empowering truth standing before you is that you possess the power to alter this narrative and regain control over your mental landscape.

The 7-Day and 14-Day Dopamine Detox Blueprints serve as pivotal resources for facilitating this transformation. The 7-day detox acts as a swift reset button, enabling you to recognize and manage distractions effectively. It's an ideal starting point for those who may be encountering this concept for the first time, providing a manageable yet impactful introduction to the principles of dopamine detoxing.

On the other hand, the 14-day blueprint offers a deeper exploration of your habits and thought processes, encouraging significant self-reflection and the development of lasting habits that promote continuous personal growth. With this enhanced understanding of how dopamine influences your cravings for instant gratification, you are now equipped and empowered to liberate yourself from the relentless cycle of distraction and redirect your focus toward your long-term ambitions.

In addition to these detox plans, establishing structured routines and environments designed to reduce interruptions is crucial for maintaining the focus and discipline we've discussed throughout this journey. This may involve designating specific time slots in your day that are dedicated to concentrated work, creating a schedule that promotes productivity without the interruptions that often derail your intentions.

Furthermore, decluttering your workspace can create a more inviting and efficient environment, reinforcing your commitment to success. It's essential to recognize that sustaining focus and discipline is not a one-time achievement but rather an ongoing journey. Regularly evaluating your progress, setting new milestones, and adjusting your strategies as needed are vital steps in this process. Additionally, surrounding yourself with supportive individuals who understand your goals can significantly enhance your journey by boosting your accountability and motivation.

As a result of these transformative changes, you will experience a life redefined through intentional living. Picture yourself accomplishing tasks you once deemed impossible, armed with newfound mental toughness and the discipline necessary to tackle challenges head-on.

You'll find that you can savor each moment fully, free from the incessant urge to check your notifications or scroll through social media feeds—creating a harmonious balance between your personal and professional spheres. This shift is not merely a vision or a distant dream; it is a tangible reality that will materialize through your continued efforts, commitment, and dedication to the process.

My ultimate goal is to help you break free from the chains of distraction by providing you with a comprehensive roadmap that guides you every step of the way. The tools, strategies, and insights offered throughout this journey are designed to empower you to take ownership of your focus and productivity.

Finally, embracing a growth mindset will play a crucial role in your transformation. When you shift the way you view challenges, you can see them as valuable opportunities for learning and growth. When faced with obstacles, approach them as moments for reflection and adjustment rather than setbacks. As you celebrate the new mindset, you are cultivating, along with the newfound clarity and confidence you achieve, you'll take immense pride in reclaiming your productivity and mental strength.

Here's to a future brimming with purpose, clarity, and the deep fulfillment that comes from achieving your goals through the intentional practice of dopamine detoxing! As you step into this new chapter of your life, know that the potential for greatness resides within you—waiting to be unleashed through your dedication to focus, resilience, and mindful engagement with the world around you. Let this journey not only change your life, but also inspire those around you to seek their paths toward clarity and intentional living.

References

Attia, N. (2017, August 4). The potential effect of technology and distractions on undergraduate students' concentration. *Pakistan Journal of Medical Sciences.* https://doi.org/10.12669/pjms.334.12560

Bromberg-Martin, E. S., Matsumoto, M., & Hikosaka, O. (2010). Dopamine in motivational control: Rewarding, aversive, and alerting. *Neuron, 68*(5), 815–834. https://doi.org/10.1016/j.neuron.2010.11.022

Center for Substance Abuse Treatment. (2018). *Chapter 7. Clinical issues, challenges, and strategies in intensive outpatient treatment.* Nih.gov; Substance Abuse and Mental Health Services Administration (US). https://www.ncbi.nlm.nih.gov/books/NBK64101/

Common reasons for relapse & how to avoid it. (2019, December 13). *Gateway Foundation.* https://www.gatewayfoundation.org/blog/triggers-in-addiction-recovery/

Desai, D., Patel, J., Saiyed, F., Upadhyay, H., Kariya, P., & Patel, J. (2024). A literature review on holistic well-being and dopamine fasting: An integrated approach. *Cureus.* https://doi.org/10.7759/cureus.61643

Dixon, E., & Lazar, A. (2020). The role of sensory changes in everyday technology use by people with mild to moderate dementia. *The 22nd International ACM SIGACCESS Conference on Computers and Accessibility.* https://doi.org/10.1145/3373625.3417000

Dopamine deficiency: Symptoms, causes & treatment. (2022, March 23). Cleveland Clinic. https://my.clevelandclinic.org/health/articles/22588-dopamine-deficiency

Dopamine detoxes don't work: Here's what to do instead. (2024, September 9). Cleveland Clinic. https://health.clevelandclinic.org/dopamine-detox

Eckert, E. (2023). The complete guide to focus time. *Supernormal.* https://www.supernormal.com/blog/how-to-schedule-focus-time

Firth, J., Torous, J., Stubbs, B., Firth, J., Steiner, G., Smith, L., Alvarez-Jimenez, M., Gleeson, J., Vancampfort, D., Armitage, C., & Sarris, J. (2019). The "online brain": How the internet may be changing our cognition. *World Psychiatry, 18*(2), 119–129. https://doi.org/10.1002/wps.20617

George, A.S. Hovan George, Baskar, D. T., & Karthikeyan, M. (2024). Reclaiming our minds: Mitigating the negative impacts of excessive doomscrolling. *Partners Universal Multidisciplinary Research Journal, 1*(3), 17–39. https://doi.org/10.5281/zenodo.13737987

Goldstein, R. Z., & Volkow, N. D. (2011). Dysfunction of the prefrontal cortex in addiction: Neuroimaging findings and clinical implications. *Nature Reviews Neuroscience, 12*(11), 652–669. https://doi.org/10.1038/nrn3119

Gould, T. J. (2010). Addiction and cognition. *Addiction Science & Clinical Practice, 5*(2), 4. https://pmc.ncbi.nlm.nih.gov/articles/PMC3120118/

Gupta, M., Gokarakonda, S. B., & Attia, F. N. (2020). Withdrawal syndromes. *PubMed; StatPearls Publishing.* https://www.ncbi.nlm.nih.gov/books/NBK459239/

Hu, E., & Nguyen, A. (2022, April 4). Too much pleasure can lead to addiction. how to break the cycle and find balance : Life kit. *NPR.org.* https://www.npr.org/2022/03/31/1090009509/addiction-how-to-break-the-cycle-and-find-balance

Lewis, R. G., Florio, E., Punzo, D., & Borrelli, E. (2021). The brain's reward system in health and disease. *Advances in Experimental Medicine and Biology, 1344*(1344), 57–69. https://doi.org/10.1007/978-3-030-81147-1_4

Master how to delay gratification and level up your life. (2025). *Mooremomentum.com.* https://mooremomentum.com/blog/master-how-to-delay-gratification-and-level-up-your-life/

Miller, K. (2019, December 30). *What is delayed gratification and how to pass the marshmallow test?* PositivePsychology.com. https://positivepsychology.com/delayed-gratification/

nadiahall5. (2024, April 22). *The role of dopamine in major depressive disorder*. Simply Neuroscience. https://www.simplyneuroscience.org/post/the-role-of-dopamine-in-major-depressive-disorder

National Library of Medicine. (2021). Chapter 2—how stimulants affect the brain and behavior. In *www.ncbi.nlm.nih.gov*. Substance Abuse and Mental Health Services Administration (US). https://www.ncbi.nlm.nih.gov/books/NBK576548/ (Original work published 1999)

NIELD, D. (2019, December 1). *Try grayscale mode to curb Your phone addiction*. Wired. https://www.wired.com/story/grayscale-ios-android-smartphone-addiction/

Oaten, J. (2024, April 26). *Combating the attention span crisis in our students*. Santa Maria College. https://santamaria.wa.edu.au/decreasing-attention-spans-jennifer-oaten/

Riaz Laghari. (2024, December 15). Mastering the phd journey: A guide to research, resilience, and excellence. *Medium.* https://medium.com/@riazleghari/mastering-the-phd-journey-a-guide-to-research-resilience-and-excellence-4387485a88bb

Scroggs, L. (2021). *The pomodoro technique — why it works & how to do it.* Todoist. https://www.todoist.com/productivity-methods/pomodoro-technique

Setia, S., Gilbert, F., Tichy, M. L., Redpath, J., Shahzad, N., & Marraccini, M. E. (2025). Digital detox strategies and mental health: A comprehensive scoping review of why, where, and how. *Cureus.* https://doi.org/10.7759/cureus.78250

Speranza, L., di Porzio, U., Viggiano, D., de Donato, A., & Volpicelli, F. (2021). Dopamine: The neuromodulator of long-term synaptic plasticity, reward and movement control. *Cells, 10*(4), 735. https://doi.org/10.3390/cells10040735

Stay focused at work: Top tips to minimize distractions. (2025, February 13). *Buttimer Consulting.* https://buttimerconsulting.com/blog/stay-focused-at-work/

Team, L. E. (2023, December 22). *Work sprints: boosting productivity and achieving results.* Larksuite.com. https://www.larksuite.com/en_us/topics/productivity-glossary/work-sprints

Volkow, N. D., Wang, G.-J., Fowler, J. S., Tomasi, D., Telang, F., & Baler, R. (2010, August 17). Addiction: Decreased reward sensitivity and increased expectation sensitivity conspire to overwhelm the brain's control circuit. *BioEssays.* https://doi.org/10.1002/bies.201000042

Yes, ADHD paralysis is a real thing, according to psychologists. *(2024). Breeze-Wellbeing.* https://breeze-wellbeing.com/blog/adhd-paralysis/

FREE BONUS FROM PEAKSTATE PROTOCOLS

Greetings!

First, thank you for reading our books.

As a welcome gift we offer the Peakstate Protocols eBook Bundle for free. Plus, you can be the first to receive new books and exclusives! <u>Remember it's 100% free to join.</u>

Simply click the link below to join.

https://www.subscribepage.com/peakstate

Keep up to date with us on:

https://peakstateprotocols.com/

OTHER BOOKS BY PEAKSTATE PROTOCOLS

- Dopamine Detox: The 7-Day Reset to Break Distractions, Reclaim Focus & Boost Productivity
- Red Light Therapy: Unlock the Hidden Power of Redlight for Pain Relief, Energy & Anti-Aging
- Methylene Blue: The Missing Key to High Performance, Mitochondrial Energy, Focus and Productivity
- Burnout Recovery: The 7-Day Reset to Beat Stress & Exhaustion, Boost Energy & Regain Mental Clarity

www.ingramcontent.com/pod-product-compliance
Lightning Source LLC
LaVergne TN
LVHW022041200926
848481LV00003B/733
9798349356322